Oliver Goldsmith, George Birkbeck Norman Hill

Goldsmith The Traveller

Edited with Introd. and Notes by George Birkbeck Hill

Oliver Goldsmith, George Birkbeck Norman Hill

Goldsmith The Traveller
Edited with Introd. and Notes by George Birkbeck Hill

ISBN/EAN: 9783337208912

Printed in Europe, USA, Canada, Australia, Japan

Cover: Foto ©Andreas Hilbeck / pixelio.de

More available books at **www.hansebooks.com**

Clarendon Press Series

GOLDSMITH

THE TRAVELLER

G. BIRKBECK HILL

London

HENRY FROWDE

Oxford University Press Warehouse

Amen Corner, E.C.

Clarendon Press Series

GOLDSMITH

THE TRAVELLER

EDITED

WITH INTRODUCTION AND NOTES

BY

GEORGE BIRKBECK HILL, D.C.L.

PEMBROKE COLLEGE, OXFORD

Oxford

AT THE CLARENDON PRESS

1888

[*All rights reserved*]

INTRODUCTION.

THE first title suggested for this beautiful poem was, we are told, *The Philosophical Wanderer*.[1] *The Wanderer* would certainly have been more pleasing to our ears than *The Traveller*; but that name was already borne by a 'moral poem' by Richard Savage, whose *Life* Johnson wrote. If, therefore, it was to be used at all, it required some such addition as *Philosophical*. Happily Goldsmith's good taste led him to reject a title which would have been altogether unworthy of his exquisite versification. He reserved it in a somewhat modified form for his *Vicar of Wakefield*; where, in the chapter entitled *The History of a Philosophic Vagabond pursuing Novelty but losing Content*, we have the prose version of one part of *The Traveller*. In 1754, when he was now in the twenty-sixth year of his age, he had left Edinburgh, where he had been studying medicine, and had begun his wanderings. He passed through the countries which he describes in *The Traveller*, supporting himself, there is every reason to believe, in much the same way as George Primrose, the Vicar's son. 'I had some knowledge of music, with a tolerable voice,' says the Philosophic Vagabond, 'and now turned what was my amusement into a present means of subsistence. I passed among the harmless peasants of Flanders, and among

---

[1] Mr. Forster (*Life of Goldsmith*, ed. 1871, i. 368) states that it was Johnson who suggested this title. His authority seems to be Prior's *Life of Goldsmith*, ii. 18; but Prior does not say this.

such of the French as were poor enough to be very merry; for I ever found them sprightly in proportion to their wants. Whenever I approached a peasant's house towards nightfall, I played one of my most merry tunes, and that procured me not only a lodging but subsistence for the next day.' When he reached Italy he says:—'My skill in music could avail me nothing in a country where every peasant was a better musician than I; but by this time I had acquired another title which answered my purpose as well, and this was a skill in disputation. In all the foreign Universities and convents there are, upon certain days, philosophical theses maintained against every adventitious disputant; for which, if the champion opposes with any dexterity, he can claim a gratuity in money, a dinner, and a bed for one night. In this manner, therefore, I fought my way towards England, walked along from city to city, examined mankind more nearly, and, if I may so express it, saw both sides of the picture.'

It is not only in *The Traveller* and *The Vicar of Wakefield* that Goldsmith has set forth the knowledge of mankind which he gained in his wanderings, and the reflections which arose in his meditative mind. In the *Enquiry into the Present State of Polite Learning*, in *The Citizen of the World*, in his minor Essays, and even in his *History of the Earth and Animated Nature*, can be seen the footprints of his pilgrimage. Of his *Traveller* Lord Macaulay says, in his admirable sketch of Goldsmith's *Life*, that 'in one respect it differs from all his other writings. In general his designs were bad, and his execution good. In *The Traveller*, the execution, though deserving of much praise, is far inferior to the design. No philosophical poem, ancient or modern, has a plan so noble, and, at the same time, so simple. An English wanderer, seated on a crag among the Alps, near the point where three great countries meet, looks down on the boundless prospect, reviews his long pilgrimage, recalls the varieties of scenery, of climate, of government, of religion, of national character, which he has observed, and comes to the conclusion, just or unjust, that our happiness depends little on political institutions, and much on the temper and regulation of our own minds.'

There is only a half-truth in what the poet teaches. Even under the most perfect system of government there must always be great unhappiness; but, on the other hand, under a thoroughly bad system there can be no great happiness. 'Luke's iron crown and Damiens' bed of steel' are indeed 'to men remote from power but rarely known'; nevertheless every house in every village may suffer from the oppression of the taxgatherer and the feudal lord. Goldsmith, in his wanderings, must have heard many a tale of the cruel wrongs suffered by the poor and weak in France and Italy. 'As soon as Dover is left behind,' wrote a shrewd observer, 'every man seems to belong to some other man, and no man to himself.'[1] 'The great,' said Johnson, 'live in France very magnificently, but the rest very miserably.'[2] The sufferings of the peasantry from exactions of all sorts, due to bad laws, cannot be hidden beneath a veil, however gracefully woven, cast over them by a poet. Yet we are charmed, and rightly charmed, by Goldsmith's verse and teaching, though we are not fully convinced. From wealth evil does spring as well as good; and it is in ourselves that happiness must mainly be found.

'And peace, oh virtue! peace is all thy own.'[3]

When we leave the philosophy of *The Traveller* on one side, and consider only the poetry, we must place it half-way between two widely different schools. It is still under the influence of

[1] Mrs. Piozzi's *Journey through France*, &c. ii. 341.
[2] *Life of Johnson*. Clarendon Press ed., ii. 402.
[3] Pope, *Essay on Man*, iv. 82.

Dryden and Pope, and therefore often conventional in the descriptions of nature. Nevertheless, the poet had a keen eye for natural beauty, and now and then ventured to shake himself free from the trammels of custom. If in his description of Italy (lines 111-122) we find nothing but what might have just as well been written by a man who had never gone beyond the sound of Bow Bells, in the lines about the Loire (243-246) and Holland (293-294) we see signs of that truer style which, in spite of the artificiality with which it is still mixed, forms so much of the charm of *The Deserted Village*. In his pictures of peasant life he has shaken himself altogether free from the shepherds and shepherdesses of the conventional poets. We have no 'dialogue of imaginary swains,' no satyrs and fauns, no naiads and dryads. It is true that the coarseness of life is too much varnished over. With Crabbe he could not have boasted—

'I paint the cot
As truth will paint it, and as bards will not.'[1]

Nevertheless, though both in *The Traveller* and *The Deserted Village* the whole effect is untrue to nature, there is to be found in them many an admirably natural touch. We may be in Arcadia, but it is the Arcadia, not of the pastoral poets of Queen Anne and the first two Georges, but of the Forest of Arden. It is men and women whom we meet, and not insipid creatures, male and female, with crooks and chaplets and alternations of sentimentality in sickly verse.

'Goldsmith,' said Johnson, 'was a plant that flowered late.'[2] He was thirty-six years old when he published *The Traveller*. The quantity of verse which he left is so small that, like his contemporary, Gray's, it can easily be read in a single evening. He wrote so little, perhaps, because he wrote so carefully.

---

[1] Crabbe's *Works*, ed. 1834, ii. 11.
[2] *Life of Johnson*, iii. 167.

Beneath the beautiful ease of his versification, the labour which he had bestowed on it is never seen. 'His prose,' we are told, 'flowed from him with such facility, that in whole quires of his *Histories*, *Animated Nature*, &c., he had seldom occasion to correct or alter a single word ; but in his verses, especially his two great ethic poems, nothing could exceed the patient and incessant revisal which he bestowed upon them. To save himself the trouble of transcription, he wrote the lines in his first copy very wide, and would so fill up the intermediate space with reiterated corrections that scarcely a word of his first effusions was left unaltered.'[1] He was but forty-five when he died. The plant that had been so late in flowering suddenly withered away when it seemed fullest of bloom.

[1] Goldsmith's *Misc. Works*, ed. 1801, i. 113.

ARGUMENT OF THE POEM.

ll. 1-22. The poet in all his wanderings turns with longings to his brother's dwelling where he had found peace.

ll. 23-30. He describes his restless pursuit of some good that ever eludes his grasp.

ll. 31-36. Seated on a crag among the Alps he begins his meditations.

ll. 37-50. He looks round on creation and he sees that it is good, however much the pride of a false philosophy may pretend to scorn each thing separately. Through sympathy he claims his share in all the good which he sees.

ll. 51-62. Yet sorrow falls upon him when he reflects how small is the stock of the happiness of men. He longs to find a spot where he may grow happy in seeing all around him happy.

ll. 63-80. He is perplexed by finding that every race maintains that with it alone the chief happiness dwells. He suspects that all have an equal share of blessings; nature or art, by the diversity of gifts, keeping the balance even.

ll. 81-98. Nature in every land alike will grant to labour all that is needful for life. Art gives her gifts more capriciously, but each blessing is accompanied by some evil peculiar to it. Each state pursues some one object too eagerly to its own hurt.

ll. 99-104. The poet takes advantage of his lofty position to follow this train of thought from nation to nation.

ll. 105-122. He begins with Italy, for which Nature has done all that Nature can do.

ll. 123-144. Yet in Italy happiness is not found, for the inhabitants, given up to the pleasures of the senses, are unworthy of the beauty amidst which they dwell. Wealth had passed over the land, and passing away had left an evil train behind.

ll. 145-164. Art comes in with its compensations, base though they are. If the heart is feeble, the mind fallen, and the soul unmanned, it supplies low delights in which they find full satisfaction.

ll. 165-174. The poet turns in disdain to a rougher climate and a ruder race—to Switzerland, for which Nature does so little.

ll. 175-198. Here there is the content which springs from the absence of envy and of wishes that can never be gratified. Labour gives health, and the enjoyment of well-earned rest at the close of every day.

ll. 199-208. The very rudeness of the climate and the soil, by heightening the enjoyment of the good things which the peasant can wring from them, endears his country still more to him.

ll. 209-226. But the very fewness of wants which gives him his content limits his happiness. To the higher pleasures of the imagination he is insensible. The only rapture of which he knows is the rapture of low debauchery.

ll. 227-238. To the refinements of life and to the delicacies of love and friendship he is insensible. He may have the sterner virtues, but he knows nothing of those gentle manners and that politeness which come from culture alone.

ll. 239-254. These are found under kinder skies—in France.

ll. 255-266. There every one tries to please, and to be pleased. Praise passes from one to the other, like current coin, whose genuineness no one cares to test; till at last all become blessed by being convinced that they are so.

ll. 267-280. But this love of praise brings with it its own evils. The weakened soul, losing its self-dependent powers, can no longer stand alone. Ostentation comes in, and vanity and beggar pride.

ll. 281-296. The poet next gives flight to his fancy, and turns towards men of solider mind, who by patient toil had won their Holland from the sea.

ll. 297-316. But industry is accompanied by too eager a love of gain. Opulence, which gives the conveniences of life, destroys at the same time its dignity and worth, and freedom is bartered for gold.

ll. 317-334. He turns his thoughts to Britain, an island favoured in the highest degree by Nature, and inhabited by the lords of the world—the home of freedom.

ll. 335-348. But freedom passes into surliness in private life and into faction in public life.

ll. 349-360. The general feeling of natural reverence decays; and its place is ill-supplied by respect for wealth. Genius and worth are slighted, and this once 'happy breed of men' seems settling down to the low level to which avarice reduces everything.

ll. 361-376. The poet, while thus pointing out the ills which spring from freedom, is far from courting the great. He loves liberty; it is license that he hates and dreads. There alone is real freedom where the thinkers govern the toilers, and where each man in each class bears his fair share of the public burthens.

ll. 377-392. In Britain factions are struggling against the King, to win not liberty, but power. The plunder of conquered nations is used to enslave Englishmen at home.

ll. 393-412. The source of the evil is to be found in the blows struck at the power of the King. Honour has yielded to wealth, and wealth, which now alone sways the mind, that it may maintain its grandeur, lays the country waste. Melancholy bands of emigrants, driven from their homes, are starting for the wilds of America.

ll. 413-422. There, in the midst of their wanderings and their dangers, they look back with longing to the country which they have left.

ll. 423 to end. The long search for happiness is idle; for if found anywhere, it is found in each man's breast. It is not in kings or laws but in ourselves that it has its spring. To few indeed does the hand of the tyrant reach; within the grasp of almost all is placed that peace which virtue gives.

THE
TRAVELLER;

OR, A

PROSPECT OF SOCIETY.

A

POEM.

INSCRIBED TO THE

REV. MR. HENRY GOLDSMITH.

BY

OLIVER GOLDSMITH, M.B.

LONDON:
Printed for J. NEWBERY, in ST. PAUL'S CHURCH-YARD.
MDCCLXV

TO THE REV. HENRY GOLDSMITH.

DEAR SIR,

I AM sensible that the friendship between us can acquire no new force from the ceremonies of a Dedication; and perhaps it demands an excuse thus to prefix your name to my attempts, which you decline giving with your own. But as a part of this Poem was formerly written to you from Switzerland, the whole can now, with propriety, be only inscribed to you. It will also throw a light upon many parts of it, when the reader understands, that it is addressed to a man, who, despising Fame and Fortune, has retired early to Happiness and Obscurity, with an income of forty pounds a year.

I now perceive, my dear brother, the wisdom of your humble choice. You have entered upon a sacred office; where the harvest is great, and the labourers are but few; while you have left the field of Ambition, where the labourers are many, and the harvest not worth carrying away. But of all kinds of ambition, what from the refinement of the times, from different systems of criticism, and from the divisions of party, that which pursues poetical fame is the wildest.

Poetry makes a principal amusement among unpolished nations; but in a country verging to the extremes of refinement, Painting and Music come in for a share. As these offer the feeble mind a less laborious entertainment, they at first rival Poetry, and at length supplant her; they engross all that favour once shown to her, and though but younger sisters, seize upon the elder's birthright.

Yet, however this art may be neglected by the powerful, it is still in greater danger from the mistaken efforts of the learned to improve it. What criticisms have we not heard of late in favour of blank verse, and Pindaric odes, choruses, anapests and iambics, alliterative care and happy negligence! Every absurdity has now a champion to defend it; and as he is generally much in the wrong, so he has always much to say; for error is ever talkative.

But there is an enemy to this art still more dangerous, I mean Party. Party entirely distorts the judgment, and destroys the taste. When the mind is once infected with this disease, it can only find pleasure in what contributes to increase the distemper. Like the tiger, that seldom desists from pursuing man after having once preyed upon human flesh, the reader, who has once gratified his appetite with calumny, makes, ever after, the most agreeable feast upon murdered reputation. Such readers generally admire some half-witted thing, who wants to be thought a bold man, having lost the character of a wise one. Him they dignify with the name of poet; his tawdry lampoons are called satires, his turbulence is said to be force, and his phrenzy fire.

What reception a Poem may find, which has neither abuse, party, nor blank verse to support it, I cannot tell, nor am I solicitous to know. My aims are right. Without espousing the cause of any party, I have attempted to moderate the rage of all. I have endeavoured to show, that there may be equal happiness in states, that are differently governed from our own; that every state has a particular principle of happiness, and that this principle in each may be carried to a mischievous excess. There are few can judge, better than yourself, how far these positions are illustrated in this Poem.

                I am, dear Sir,
           Your most affectionate Brother,
                        OLIVER GOLDSMITH.

THE TRAVELLER;

OR,

A PROSPECT OF SOCIETY.

  Remote, unfriended, melancholy, slow,
Or by the lazy Scheldt, or wandering Po;
Or onward, where the rude Carinthian boor,
Against the houseless stranger shuts the door;
5 Or where Campania's plain forsaken lies,
A weary waste expanding to the skies:
Where'er I roam, whatever realms to see,
My heart untravell'd fondly turns to thee;
Still to my brother turns, with ceaseless pain,
10 And drags at each remove a lengthening chain.

  Eternal blessings crown my earliest friend,
And round his dwelling guardian saints attend:
Bless'd be that spot, where cheerful guests retire
To pause from toil, and trim their ev'ning fire;
15 Bless'd that abode, where want and pain repair,
And every stranger finds a ready chair;
Bless'd be those feasts with simple plenty crown'd,
Where all the ruddy family around
Laugh at the jests or pranks that never fail,
20 Or sigh with pity at some mournful tale,
Or press the bashful stranger to his food,
And learn the luxury of doing good.

But me, not destin'd such delights to share,
My prime of life in wand'ring spent and care,
25 Impell'd, with steps unceasing, to pursue
Some fleeting good, that mocks me with the view
That, like the circle bounding earth and skies,
Allures from far, yet, as I follow, flies;
My fortune leads to travel realms alone,
30 And find no spot of all the world my own.

Even now, where Alpine solitudes ascend,
I sit me down a pensive hour to spend;
And, plac'd on high above the storm's career,
Look downward where an hundred realms appear:
35 Lakes, forests, cities, plains, extending wide,
The pomp of kings, the shepherd's humbler pride.

When thus Creation's charms around combine,
Amidst the store, should thankless pride repine?
Say, should the philosophic mind disdain
40 That good, which makes each humbler bosom vain?
Let school-taught pride dissemble all it can,
These little things are great to little man;
And wiser he, whose sympathetic mind
Exults in all the good of all mankind.
45 Ye glitt'ring towns, with wealth and splendour crown'd.
Ye fields, where summer spreads profusion round,
Ye lakes, whose vessels catch the busy gale,
Ye bending swains, that dress the flow'ry vale,
For me your tributary stores combine;
50 Creation's heir, the world, the world is mine!

As some lone miser visiting his store,
Bends at his treasure, counts, re-counts it o'er;
Hoards after hoards his rising raptures fill,
Yet still he sighs, for hoards are wanting still:
55 Thus to my breast alternate passions rise,
Pleas'd with each good that heaven to man supplies:
Yet oft a sigh prevails, and sorrows fall,
To see the hoard of human bliss so small;
And oft I wish, amidst the scene, to find
60 Some spot to real happiness consign'd,
Where my worn soul, each wand'ring hope at rest,
May gather bliss to see my fellows bless'd.

But where to find that happiest spot below,
Who can direct, when all pretend to know?
65 The shudd'ring tenant of the frigid zone
Boldly proclaims that happiest spot his own,
Extols the treasures of his stormy seas,
And his long nights of revelry and ease;
The naked negro, panting at the line,
70 Boasts of his golden sands and palmy wine,
Basks in the glare, or stems the tepid wave,
And thanks his Gods for all the good they gave.
Such is the patriot's boast, where'er we roam,
His first, best country ever is, at home.
75 And yet, perhaps, if countries we compare,
And estimate the blessings which they share,
Though patriots flatter, still shall wisdom find
An equal portion dealt to all mankind,

As different good, by Art or Nature given,
80 To different nations makes their blessings even.

Nature, a mother kind alike to all,
Still grants her bliss at Labour's earnest call:
With food as well the peasant is supplied
On Idra's cliffs as Arno's shelvy side;
85 And though the rocky crested summits frown,
These rocks, by custom, turn to beds of down.
From Art more various are the blessings sent:
Wealth, commerce, honour, liberty, content.
Yet these each other's power so strong contest,
90 That either seems destructive of the rest.
Where wealth and freedom reign contentment fails,
And honour sinks where commerce long prevails.
Hence every state to one lov'd blessing prone,
Conforms and models life to that alone.
95 Each to the favourite happiness attends,
And spurns the plan that aims at other ends;
Till, carried to excess in each domain,
This favourite good begets peculiar pain.

But let us try these truths with closer eyes.
100 And trace them through the prospect as it lies:
Here for a while my proper cares resign'd,
Here let me sit in sorrow for mankind,
Like yon neglected shrub at random cast,
That shades the steep, and sighs at every blast.

105 Far to the right where Apennine ascends,
Bright as the summer, Italy extends;

Its uplands sloping deck the mountain's side,
Woods over woods in gay theatric pride;
While oft some temple's mould'ring tops between
With venerable grandeur mark the scene.

Could Nature's bounty satisfy the breast,
The sons of Italy were surely blest.
Whatever fruits in different climes were found,
That proudly rise, or humbly court the ground;
Whatever blooms in torrid tracts appear,
Whose bright succession decks the varied year;
Whatever sweets salute the northern sky
With vernal lives that blossom but to die;
These here disporting own the kindred soil,
Nor ask luxuriance from the planter's toil;
While sea-born gales their gelid wings expand
To winnow fragrance round the smiling land.

But small the bliss that sense alone bestows,
And sensual bliss is all the nation knows.
In florid beauty groves and fields appear,
Man seems the only growth that dwindles here.
Contrasted faults through all his manners reign,
Though poor, luxurious, though submissive, vain,
Though grave, yet trifling, zealous, yet untrue;
And e'en in penance planning sins anew.
All evils here contaminate the mind,
That opulence departed leaves behind;
For wealth was theirs, not far remov'd the date,
When commerce proudly flourish'd through the state;

135 At her command the palace learn'd to rise,
Again the long-fall'n column sought the skies;
. The canvas glow'd beyond e'en Nature warm,
The pregnant quarry teem'd with human form;
Till, more unsteady than the southern gale,
140 Commerce on other shores display'd her sail;
While nought remain'd of all that riches gave,
But towns unmann'd, and lords without a slave;
And late the nation found with fruitless skill
Its former strength was but plethoric ill.

145   Yet still the loss of wealth is here supplied
By arts, the splendid wrecks of former pride;
From these the feeble heart and long-fall'n mind
An easy compensation seem to find.
Here may be seen, in bloodless pomp array'd,
150 The paste-board triumph and the cavalcade;
Processions form'd for piety and love,
A mistress or a saint in every grove.
By sports like these are all their cares beguil'd,
The sports of children satisfy the child;
155 Each nobler aim, represt by long control,
Now sinks at last, or feebly mans the soul;
While low delights, succeeding fast behind,
In happier meanness occupy the mind:
As in those domes, where Caesars once bore sway,
160 Defac'd by time and tottering in decay,
There in the ruin, heedless of the dead,
The shelter-seeking peasant builds his shed,

And, wond'ring man could want the larger pile,
Exults, and owns his cottage with a smile.

165 My soul, turn from them, turn we to survey
Where rougher climes a nobler race display,
Where the bleak Swiss their stormy mansions tread,
And force a churlish soil for scanty bread;
No product here the barren hills afford,
170 But man and steel, the soldier and his sword.
No vernal blooms their torpid rocks array,
But winter ling'ring chills the lap of May;
No Zephyr fondly sues the mountain's breast,
But meteors glare, and stormy glooms invest.

175 Yet still, ev'n here, content can spread a charm,
Redress the clime, and all its rage disarm.
Though poor the peasant's hut, his feast though small,
He sees his little lot the lot of all;
Sees no contiguous palace rear its head
180 To shame the meanness of his humble shed;
No costly lord the sumptuous banquet deal,
To make him loathe his vegetable meal;
But calm, and bred in ignorance and toil,
Each wish contracting, fits him to the soil.
185 Cheerful at morn he wakes from short repose,
Breasts the keen air, and carols as he goes;
With patient angle trolls the finny deep,
Or drives his venturous ploughshare to the steep,
Or seeks the den where snow-tracks mark the way,
190 And drags the struggling savage into day.

At night returning, every labour sped,
He sits him down the monarch of a shed :
Smiles by his cheerful fire, and round surveys
His children's looks, that brighten at the blaze ;
195 While his lov'd partner, boastful of her hoard,
Displays her cleanly platter on the board :
And haply too some pilgrim, thither led,
With many a tale repays the nightly bed.

Thus every good his native wilds impart,
200 Imprints the patriot passion on his heart,
And ev'n those ills, that round his mansion rise,
Enhance the bliss his scanty fund supplies.
Dear is that shed to which his soul conforms,
And dear that hill which lifts him to the storms ;
205 And as a child, when scaring sounds molest,
Clings close and closer to the mother's breast,
So the loud torrent, and the whirlwind's roar,
But bind him to his native mountains more.

Such are the charms to barren states assigned ;
210 Their wants but few, their wishes all confin'd.
Yet let them only share the praises due,
If few their wants, their pleasures are but few ;
For every want that stimulates the breast
Becomes a source of pleasure when redrest.
215 Whence from such lands each pleasing science flies,
That first excites desire, and then supplies ;
Unknown to them, when sensual pleasures cloy,
To fill the languid pause with finer joy :

Unknown those powers that raise the soul to flame,
220 Catch every nerve, and vibrate through the frame.
Their level life is but a smould'ring fire,
Unquench'd by want, unfann'd by strong desire;
Unfit for raptures, or, if raptures cheer
On some high festival of once a year,
225 In wild excess the vulgar breast takes fire,
Till, buried in debauch, the bliss expire.

But not their joys alone thus coarsely flow:
Their morals, like their pleasures, are but low,
For, as refinement stops, from sire to son
230 Unalter'd, unimprov'd, the manners run;
And love's and friendship's finely-pointed dart
Fall blunted from each indurated heart.
Some sterner virtues o'er the mountain's breast
May sit, like falcons cow'ring on the nest;
235 But all the gentler morals, such as play
Through life's more cultur'd walks, and charm the way,
These far dispers'd, on timorous pinions fly,
To sport and flutter in a kinder sky.

To kinder skies, where gentler manners reign,
240 I turn; and France displays her bright domain.
Gay sprightly land of mirth and social ease,
Pleas'd with thyself, whom all the world can please,
How often have I led thy sportive choir,
With tuneless pipe, beside the murmuring Loire?
245 Where shading elms along the margin grew,
And freshen'd from the wave the Zephyr flew:

And haply, though my harsh touch faltering still,
But mock'd all tune, and marr'd the dancer's skill;
Yet would the village praise my wondrous power,
250 And dance, forgetful of the noon-tide hour.
Alike all ages. Dames of ancient days
Have led their children through the mirthful maze,
And the gay grandsire, skill'd in gestic lore,
Has frisk'd beneath the burthen of threescore.

255 So bless'd a life these thoughtless realms display,
Thus idly busy rolls their world away:
Theirs are those arts that mind to mind endear,
For honour forms the social temper here:
Honour, that praise which real merit gains,
260 Or ev'n imaginary worth obtains,
Here passes current; paid from hand to hand,
It shifts in splendid traffic round the land:
From courts, to camps, to cottages it strays,
And all are taught an avarice of praise;
265 They please, are pleas'd, they give to get esteem,
Till, seeming bless'd, they grow to what they seem.

But while this softer art their bliss supplies,
It gives their follies also room to rise;
For praise too dearly lov'd, or warmly sought,
270 Enfeebles all internal strength of thought;
And the weak soul, within itself unblest,
Leans for all pleasure on another's breast.
Hence ostentation here, with tawdry art,
Pants for the vulgar praise which fools impart;

275 Here vanity assumes her pert grimace,
　　And trims her robes of frieze with copper lace:
　　Here beggar pride defrauds her daily cheer,
　　To boast one splendid banquet once a year;
　　The mind still turns where shifting fashion draws,
280 Nor weighs the solid worth of self-applause.

　　To men of other minds my fancy flies,
　　Embosom'd in the deep where Holland lies.
　　Methinks her patient sons before me stand,
　　Where the broad ocean leans against the land,
285 And, sedulous to stop the coming tide,
　　Lift the tall rampire's artificial pride.
　　Onward, methinks, and diligently slow,
　　The firm-connected bulwark seems to grow;
　　Spreads its long arms amidst the wat'ry roar,
290 Scoops out an empire, and usurps the shore.
　　While the pent ocean rising o'er the pile,
　　Sees an amphibious world beneath him smile:
　　The slow canal, the yellow-blossom'd vale,
　　The willow-tufted bank, the gliding sail,
295 The crowded mart, the cultivated plain,
　　A new creation rescu'd from his reign.

　　Thus, while around the wave-subjected soil
　　Impels the native to repeated toil,
　　Industrious habits in each bosom reign,
300 And industry begets a love of gain.
　　Hence all the good from opulence that springs,
　　With all those ills superfluous treasure brings,

Are here displayed. Their much-lov'd wealth imparts
Convenience, plenty, elegance, and arts;
305 But view them closer, craft and fraud appear,
Ev'n liberty itself is barter'd here.
At gold's superior charms all freedom flies,
The needy sell it, and the rich man buys;
A land of tyrants, and a den of slaves,
310 Here wretches seek dishonourable graves,
And calmly bent, to servitude conform,
Dull as their lakes that slumber in the storm.

Heavens! how unlike their Belgic sires of old!
Rough, poor, content, ungovernably bold;
315 War in each breast, and freedom on each brow;
How much unlike the sons of Britain now!

Fir'd at the sound, my genius spreads her wing,
And flies where Britain courts the western spring;
Where lawns extend that scorn Arcadian pride,
320 And brighter streams than fam'd Hydaspes glide.
There all around the gentlest breezes stray,
There gentle music melts on every spray;
Creation's mildest charms are there combin'd,
Extremes are only in the master's mind!
325 Stern o'er each bosom reason holds her state,
With daring aims irregularly great,
Pride in their port, defiance in their eye,
I see the lords of human kind pass by,
Intent on high designs, a thoughtful band,
330 By forms unfashion'd, fresh from Nature's hand;

Fierce in their native hardiness of soul.
True to imagin'd right, above control,
While ev'n the peasant boasts these rights to scan,
And learns to venerate himself as man.

335 Thine, Freedom, thine the blessings pictur'd here,
Thine are those charms that dazzle and endear;
Too bless'd, indeed, were such without alloy,
But foster'd ev'n by Freedom ills annoy:
That independence Britons prize too high,
340 Keeps man from man, and breaks the social tie;
The self-dependent lordlings stand alone,
All claims that bind and sweeten life unknown;
Here by the bonds of nature feebly held,
Minds combat minds, repelling and repell'd.
345 Ferments arise, imprison'd factions roar,
Repress'd ambition struggles round her shore,
Till over-wrought, the general system feels
Its motions stop, or phrenzy fire the wheels.

Nor this the worst. As nature's ties decay,
350 As duty, love, and honour fail to sway,
Fictitious bonds, the bonds of wealth and law,
Still gather strength, and force unwilling awe.
Hence all obedience bows to these alone,
And talent sinks, and merit weeps unknown;
355 Till time may come, when stripp'd of all her charms,
The land of scholars, and the nurse of arms,
Where noble stems transmit the patriot flame,
Where kings have toil'd, and poets wrote for fame,

One sink of level avarice shall lie,
360 And scholars, soldiers, kings, unhonour'd die.

 Yet think not, thus when Freedom's ills I state,
I mean to flatter kings, or court the great;
Ye powers of truth, that bid my soul aspire,
Far from my bosom drive the low desire;
365 And thou, fair Freedom, taught alike to feel
The rabble's rage, and tyrant's angry steel;
Thou transitory flower, alike undone
By proud contempt, or favour's fostering sun,
Still may thy blooms the changeful clime endure,
370 I only would repress them to secure:
For just experience tells, in every soil,
That those who think must govern those that toil;
And all that freedom's highest aims can reach,
Is but to lay proportion'd loads on each.
375 Hence, should one order disproportion'd grow,
Its double weight must ruin all below.

 O then how blind to all that earth requires,
Who think it freedom when a part aspires!
Calm is my soul, nor apt to rise in arms,
380 Except when fast-approaching danger warms:
But when contending chiefs blockade the throne,
Contracting regal power to stretch their own,
When I behold a factious band agree
To call it freedom when themselves are free;
385 Each wanton judge new penal statutes draw,
Laws grind the poor, and rich men rule the law;

The wealth of climes, where savage nations roam,
Pillag'd from slaves to purchase slaves at home;
Fear, pity, justice, indignation start,
390 Tear off reserve, and bare my swelling heart;
Till half a patriot, half a coward grown,
I fly from petty tyrants to the throne.

Yes, brother, curse with me that baleful hour,
When first ambition struck at regal power;
395 And thus polluting honour in its source,
Gave wealth to sway the mind with double force.
Have we not seen, round Britain's peopled shore,
Her useful sons exchanged for useless ore?
Seen all her triumphs but destruction haste,
400 Like flaring tapers brightening as they waste;
Seen opulence, her grandeur to maintain,
Lead stern depopulation in her train,
And over fields where scatter'd hamlets rose,
In barren solitary pomp repose?
405 Have we not seen at pleasure's lordly call,
The smiling long-frequented village fall?
Beheld the duteous son, the sire decay'd,
The modest matron, and the blushing maid,
Forc'd from their homes, a melancholy train,
410 To traverse climes beyond the western main;
Where wild Oswego spreads her swamps around.
And Niagara stuns with thund'ring sound?

Even now, perhaps, as there some pilgrim strays
Through tangled forests, and through dangerous ways;

415 Where beasts with man divided empire claim,
    And the brown Indian marks with murderous aim;
    There, while above the giddy tempest flies,
    And all around distressful yells arise,
    The pensive exile, bending with his woe,
420 To stop too fearful, and too faint to go,
    Casts a long look where England's glories shine,
    And bids his bosom sympathise with mine.

    Vain, very vain, my weary search to find
    That bliss which only centres in the mind:
425 Why have I stray'd from pleasure and repose,
    To seek a good each government bestows?
    In every government, though terrors reign,
    Though tyrant kings, or tyrant laws restrain,
    How small, of all that human hearts endure,
430 That part which laws or kings can cause or cure.
    Still to ourselves in every place consign'd,
    Our own felicity we make or find:
    With secret course, which no loud storms annoy,
    Glides the smooth current of domestic joy.
435 The lifted axe, the agonising wheel,
    Luke's iron crown, and Damiens' bed of steel,
    To men remote from power but rarely known,
    Leave reason, faith, and conscience, all our own.

NOTES.[1]

DEDICATION.

HENRY GOLDSMITH was some years older than Oliver. He was at this time curate of Kilkenny West, in Longford; living in the farmhouse in which he and his brother had been born. He died in May 1768. In the Dedication of *The Deserted Village* to Reynolds, Goldsmith says:—
'The only dedication I ever made was to my brother, because I loved him better than most other men. He is since dead. Permit me to inscribe this Poem to you.' In the character of the village preacher in that poem we have a portrait in which are blended the poet's father and brother. To address his brother in a Dedication as 'Dear Sir' was agreeable to the greater formality of the age. He uses the same address even in a private letter. See Forster's *Life of Goldsmith*, ed. 1871, i. 164.

The title of *The Philosophical Wanderer* was first suggested for the poem.—Prior's *Life of Goldsmith*, ii. 18. See *The Vicar of Wakefield*, ch. 20, for the history of a philosophic vagabond.

l. 5. It was as early as February, 1756, that Goldsmith returned from his travels. In one part of his poems therefore he complied with Horace's rule—'nonumque prematur in annum.'—*Ars Poet.* l. 388.

---

[1] In these notes I have drawn, without particular acknowledgment in each case, on Prior's *Life of Goldsmith*, and the editions of Goldsmith's *Poems* by Mr. Peter Cunningham and Mr. Austin Dobson.

l. 10.
> 'A man he was to all the country dear,
> And passing rich with forty pounds a year.'
>> *Deserted Village*, l. 141

'The profits of my living,' says the Vicar of Wakefield, 'amounted to but thirty-five pounds a year.'—Ch. 2. His second cure was but 'of fifteen pounds a year.'—Ch. 3. Of Parson Adams, in Fielding's *Joseph Andrews*, we are told:—'that at the age of fifty he was provided with a handsome income of twenty-three pounds a year; which, however, he could not make any great figure with, because he lived in a dear country, and was a little encumbered with a wife and six children.'—Bk. i. ch. 3.

l. 12. 'The harvest truly is great, but the labourers are few.'—*Luke* x. 2.

l. 15. In the first edition this passage ran as follows:— 'But of all kinds of ambition, as things are now circumstanced, perhaps that which pursues poetical fame is the wildest. What from the encreased refinement of the times, from the diversity of judgments produced by opposing systems of criticism, and from the more prevalent divisions of opinion influenced by party, the strongest and happiest efforts can expect to please but in a very narrow circle. Though the poet were as sure of his aim as the imperial archer of antiquity, who boasted that he never missed the heart, yet would many of his shafts now fly at random, for the heart is too often in the wrong place.' Mr. Austin Dobson, *Life of Goldsmith*, p. 97, describing this as 'a passage evidently dictated by the half-hopeful doubt of success,' adds that 'it was quietly dropped out of the subsequent editions, its anticipations, in the face of the favour with which the poem was received, being no longer appropriate.' The 'imperial archer' was perhaps the Roman Emperor Commodus, of whom Gibbon says:—'whether he aimed at the head or heart of the animal, the wound was alike certain and mortal.'

l. 19. Johnson, in *The Idler*, No. 34, had described poetry and painting as 'two arts which pursue the same end, by the operation of the same mental faculties, and which differ only as the one represents things by marks permanent and natural, the other by signs accidental and arbitrary. The one therefore is more easily and generally understood, since similitude of form is immediately perceived; the other is capable of conveying more ideas, for men have thought and spoken of many things which they do not see.' Dryden, in his *Lines to Sir Godfrey Kneller*, says:—

' But poets are confined in narrower space,
To speak the language of their native place;
The painter widely stretches his command;
Thy pencil speaks the tongue of every land.'

It is not wonderful, therefore, that the painter and the musician are everywhere rewarded far above the poet. They have a twofold advantage. In the first place they provide entertainment for the larger numbers in their own country; for feeble minds are everywhere as common as strong ones are uncommon. In the second place they are stopped by no barriers of race and language. Goldsmith, perhaps, is the first who clearly pointed out what is one of the chief causes of the decline of poetry.

l. 25.

' Our arts are sisters, though not twins in birth,
For hymns were sung in Eden's happy earth;
But oh, the painter Muse, though last in place,
Has seized the blessing first, like Jacob's race.'
                            Lines to Sir Godfrey Kneller.

'l. 29. *blank verse.* ' From a desire in the critic of grafting the spirit of ancient languages upon the English have proceeded of late several disagreeable instances of pedantry. Among the number I think we may reckon blank verse. Nothing but the greatest sublimity of subject can render such a measure pleasing; however we now see it used upon the most trivial occasions.'—Goldsmith's *Present State of Polite Learning*, ch. xi. Johnson liked blank verse as little as Goldsmith. ' Speaking of Dodsley's *Public Virtue, a Poem*, he said, "It was fine blank," meaning to express his usual contempt for blank verse.'—*Life of Johnson*, iv. 20. Of Shenstone's poems in that measure he said:—'Those that can read them may probably find them to be like the blank verses of his neighbours.'—Johnson's *Works*, viii. 414. Gray, says the Rev. Norton Nicholls, 'disliked all poetry in blank verse except Milton.'—Gray's *Works*, ed. 1858, v. 36. Among the poets of Goldsmith's time who had written in blank verse were Akenside, Dyer, Grainger, Lyttelton, Mallet, Thomson, Young, and Watts.

Pindaric odes. Johnson, in his *Life of Cowley*, describes how that poet 'made a bold and vigorous attempt to recover' that 'lost invention of antiquity,' the Pindaric Ode. He goes on to say that 'Pindarism prevailed about half a century; but at last died gradually away, and other imitations supply its place.' He describes it as 'our Pindarick infatuation' (*Life of Prior*); 'our Pindarick madness' (*Life of Congreve*); and 'the Pindarick folly' (*Life of Watts*).

anapests and iambics.

'Ĭāmbĭcs mārch frŏm shŏrt tŏ lōng;—
  Wĭth ă lĕap ănd ă boūnd thĕ swĭft ānăpæ̆sts thrōng.'
                              Coleridge's *Metrical Feet*.'

l. 33. Goldsmith, in his *Present State of Polite Learning*, ch. xi, laughs at 'the affected security of our odes, the tuneless flow of our blank verse, the pompous epithet, laboured diction, and every other deviation from common sense, which procures the poet the applause of the month; he is praised by all, read by a few, and soon forgotten.' In his *Life of Parnell* he calls the poets of the day 'misguided innovators,' who 'vainly imagine that the more their writings are unlike prose, the more they resemble poetry.' It was Gray, and the poets of his school, whom Goldsmith thus attacked. Johnson describes Gray's *Progress of Poetry* and *The Bard* as 'two compositions at which the readers of poetry were at first content to gaze in mute amazement. Some that tried them confessed their inability to understand them. . . . Some hardy champions undertook to rescue them from neglect; and in a short time many were content to be shown beauties which they could not see.' He liked as little as Goldsmith Gray's 'alliterative care.' In criticising *The Bard* he says :—'The initial resemblances, or alliterations, "ruin, ruthless, helm or hauberk," are below the grandeur of a poem that endeavours at sublimity.'

l. 44. When, shortly after the accession of George III, William Pitt, the Great Commoner, as he was fondly called, had to retire from office before the young king's Scotch favourite, the Earl of Bute, the anger of the nation broke out in the hootings of mobs, and in the bitterest of satires, both in prose and verse. By far the ablest of the writers was Charles Churchill, who suddenly shot up in the poetic sky, for a brief hour was 'lord of the ascendant,' and then as suddenly set. He is the 'half-witted thing,' the great lampooner, whom Goldsmith thus lampoons. He had died at Calais a few weeks before the publication of *The Traveller*. On Nov. 15, 1764, Horace Walpole wrote :—'Churchill the poet is dead,—to the great joy of the Ministry and the Scotch.'—*Letters*, iv. 291. It is possible that Goldsmith's Dedication was printed before the news reached London. So far, however, was he from regretting the violence of his attack, that in the sixth edition he added 'tawdry' to 'lampoons.' 'Johnson,' says Boswell, 'talked very contemptuously of Churchill's poetry, observing that "it had a temporary currency, only from its audacity of abuse, and being filled with living names, and that it would sink into oblivion."' —*Life of Johnson*, i. 418. Cowper, on the other hand, 'had a higher opinion of Churchill than of any other contemporary writer. "It is a great thing," he said, "to be indeed a poet, and does not happen to more than one man in a century; but Churchill, the great Churchill, deserved that name." He made him, more than any other writer, his model.'— Southey's *Cowper*, i. 87, 8. In a review of *The Traveller* in the December number of *The Gentleman's Magazine* for 1764, the writer speaks of 'the crude and virulent rhapsodies upon which caprice and faction have lavished an unbounded praise, that, if known to any future time, will disgrace the present.'

On the other hand, the reviewer in *The St. James's Chronicle*, Feb. 7-9, 1765 (quoted in Prior's *Life of Goldsmith*, ii. 54), referring to Churchill's death, says : 'We think it no mean acknowledgment of the excellencies of this poem to say that, like the stars, they appear the more brilliant now that *the sun of our poetry is gone down.*'

l. 50. Johnson said :—'I would not give half a guinea to live under one form of government rather than another. It is of no moment to the happiness of an individual.'—*Life of Johnson*, ii. 170. The same thought is expressed in the lines which he wrote as a conclusion to *The Traveller.*

THE POEM.

l. 1. *slow.* Dr. Johnson said that 'Mr. Chamier once asked Goldsmith what he meant by *slow*, the last word in the first line of *The Traveller.* Did he mean tardiness of locomotion? Goldsmith, who would say something without consideration, answered, "Yes." I was sitting by, and said, "No, Sir; you do not mean tardiness of locomotion; you mean that sluggishness of mind which comes upon a man in solitude." Chamier believed then that I had written the line as much as if he had seen me write it.'—*Life of Johnson*, iii. 253. Upon this Mr. Forster remarks :—'Who can doubt that he also meant slowness of motion? The first point of the picture is *that.* The poet is moving slowly, his tardiness of gait measuring the heaviness of heart, the pensive spirit, the melancholy, of which it is the outward expression and sign.'—*Life of Goldsmith*, i. 369. Thomson, *Castle of Indolence*, i. 58, has ' sauntering and slow.'

l. 2. *wandering Po.* Goldsmith's simplicity contrasts well with Addison's embellishments, who in his *Letter from Italy* says : —
> 'Fired with a thousand raptures I survey
> Eridanus through flowery meadows stray.'

l. 3. The poet, being asked why he censured the Carinthians, 'gave as a reason his being once, after a fatiguing day's walk, obliged to quit a house he had entered for shelter, and pass part or the whole of the night in seeking another.'—Prior's *Goldsmith*, i. 192.

l. 3-4. This is one of the six couplets in the poem with imperfect rhymes; the others are lines 21-22; 79-80; 151-152; 243-244; 379-380. Of these six, four are perfect to the eye. Even Pope and Gray were far less accurate in this respect.

l. 5. 'We may reckon,' says Addison, 'by a very moderate computation, more inhabitants in the Campania of old Rome than are now in all Italy.'—Addison's *Works*, ed. 1862, i. 419.

l. 8. *untravelled*. *Untravelled* means (1) never trodden by passengers, (2) having never seen foreign countries. It is objected that there is a contradiction between this line and the tenth. But it is scarcely noticed, unless it is pointed out.

l. 10. *chain*. 'SABINA. You have left your heart behind with Florimel; we know it. CELADON. You know you wrong me; when I am with Florimel 'tis still your prisoner; it only draws a longer chain after it.'—Dryden, *Secret Love*, v. 1. 'The farther I travel I feel the pain of separation with stronger force; those ties that bind me to my native country and you are still unbroken. By every remove, I only drag a greater length of chain.'—*Citizen of the World*, Letter 3.

l. 14. *trim their ev'ning fire*. *Trim* is not used of a fire, so far as I know, by any author earlier than Goldsmith. He uses it again in *The Hermit*, st. xii.:—

'The Hermit trimm'd his little fire.'

Percy, in *The Hermit of Warksworth*, has 'mends his little fire.'

l. 21. 'Garth, in his poem on Claremont, says of the Druids :—

"Hard was their lodging, homely was their food,
For all their luxury was doing good."'

l. 24. *My prime of life*. Johnson defines *prime* as 'the spring of life; the height of health, strength, or beauty.' Cf. *Richard III*, act v. sc. 3 :—'Think, how thou stab'dst me in my prime of youth.'

l. 27. 'Death, the only friend of the wretched, for a little while mocks the weary traveller with the view, and like his horizon still flies before him.'—*Vicar of Wakefield*, ch. 29. Pope, *Essay on Man*, iv. 5, describes happiness as that

'Which still so near us, yet beyond us lies.'

Compare Goldsmith's *Hermit*, l. 7 :—

'Where wilds immeasurably spread
Seem length'ning as I go.'

l. 30.
'My destined miles I shall have gone,
By Thames or Maese, by Po or Rhone,
And found no foot of earth my own.'
Prior, *Lines written in Robe's Geography*.

Goldsmith, in *The Bee*, No. 1, writing as a traveller, had said :—'When will my wanderings be at an end? When will my restless disposition give me leave to enjoy the present hour? When at Lyons, I thought all happiness lay beyond the Alps; when in Italy, I found myself still in want of something, and expected to leave solicitude behind me by going into Romelia, and now you find me turning back, still expecting ease everywhere but where I am.'

l. 33.
'As some tall cliff, that lifts its awful form,
Swells from the vale, and midway leaves the storm,
Though round its breast the rolling clouds are spread,
Eternal sunshine settles on its head.'
The Deserted Village, l. 189.

l. 34. Cf. *Paradise Regained*, iii. 251, where the tempter

'took
The Son of God up to a mountain high.'

Of the extensive view of the Traveller, embracing as it did 'an hundred realms,' we might say with Milton :—

'By what strange parallax or optick skill
Of vision, multiply'd through air, or glass
Of telescope, were curious to enquire.'—*Ib*. iv. 40.

There were, however, more sovereign states to be seen than at present. 'The Lake of Geneva,' says Addison, 'has five different states bordering on it, the Kingdom of France, and the Duchy of Savoy, the Canton of Berne, the Bishopric of Sion, and the Republic of Geneva. I have seen papers fixed up in the Canton of Berne with this magnificent preface:—"Whereas we have been informed of several abuses committed in our ports and harbours on the Lake,'" &c.—Addison's *Works*, i. 510.

l. 41. *school-taught pride.* Mr. Pattison, in a note on Pope's *Essay on Man*, ii. 81—'Let subtle schoolmen,' &c., says:—' In the narrower sense *schoolmen* means the philosophic divines of the middle ages. Here it is to be taken in the wider sense, all who treat of morals in a technical way proper for the schools and not for the public.' *Schools* in this sense is much the same as *University*.

l. 42. 'The main of life is composed of small incidents and petty occurrences.'—*The Rambler*, No. 68.

l. 44. 'Homo sum, humani nihil a me alienum puto.'-Terence, *Heaut.* i. i. 25.

l. 47. *the busy gale.* The poet, in l. 2, had spoken of 'the lazy Scheldt.' The river, slowly bearing along the barges on its sluggish current, seemed lazy, just as the gale, driving along the vessels, seemed busy. In *The Deserted Village*, l. 11, he has 'the busy mill.' Cf. Shakespeare, *Henry V*, Act iv. Chorus, 'With busy hammers closing rivets up.'

l. 49.

'Ask for what end the heav'nly bodies shine,
Earth for whose use? Pride answers, "'Tis for mine!"
For me kind nature wakes her genial pow'r,
Suckles each herb, and spreads out ev'ry flower.'
Pope, *Essay on Man*, i. 131.

l. 50. 'More than ever was he here, in the practical paths of life, a loiterer and laggard ; yet as he passed from place to place, finding for his foot no solid resting-ground, no spot of all the world that he might hope to call his own, there was yet sinking deep into the heart of the homeless vagrant that power and possession to which all else on earth subserves and is obedient, and which out of the very abyss of poverty and want gave him right and title over all.'--Forster's *Gold-*

smith, i. 70. He was like St. Paul, 'as having nothing, and yet possessing all things' (2 *Corinthians* vi. 10); but it was by the force of his imaginative genius that he possessed them. Compare:—

'I the heir of all the ages, in the foremost files of time.'
Tennyson, *Locksley Hall*.

l. 55. The poet, looking upon himself as creation's heir, and like a miser counting his hoard, is as much grieved at what is wanting as pleased with what is present.

l. 62.
'And in proportion as it blesses blest.'
Essay on Man, iii. 300.

l. 63. Pope, addressing happiness, says:—

'Plant of celestial seed! if dropt below,
Say, in what mortal soil thou deign'st to grow?'
Essay on Man, iv. 7.

l. 70. *palmy wine*. Wine made from the juice of the palm. Johnson defines *palmy*, 'bearing palms.'

l. 78.
'Fix'd to no spot is happiness sincere,
'Tis nowhere to be found, or ev'rywhere.'
Pope, *Essay on Man*, iv. 15.

'Heav'n to mankind impartial we confess,
If all are equal in their happiness.' *Ib*. l. 53.

'And mourn our various portions as we please,
Equal is common sense and common ease.' *Ib*. l. 77.

'Alike to all, the kind impartial Heaven
The sparks of truth and happiness has giv'n.'
Gray, *Education and Government*, l. 28.

l. 84. *Idra*. It is not likely that the poet is speaking of Idra, or Idria, in Illyria, the Botany Bay of Austria. Its quicksilver mines, 'those dreadful caverns, where thousands, shut out from all hope of ever seeing the cheerful light of the sun, toil out a miserable life under the whips of task-masters,' are described in the *Gentleman's Magazine* for 1767, p. 251, and in Goldsmith's *Animated Nature*, ed. 1779, i. 79. He must mean, I think, Lake Idro in North Italy. Its shores are rocky cliffs.

shelvy side. Johnson defines *shelvy* as 'shallow; rocky; full of banks'; and gives as an instance, 'I had been drowned but that the shore was shelvy and shallow.'—*Merry Wives of Windsor*, iii. 5. Goldsmith here seems to mean that the side of the Arno rose in shelves or terraces on which the vine could be cultivated and crops grown.

l. 86. *beds of down.*

'The tyrant custom, most grave senators,
Hath made the flinty and steel couch of war
My thrice-driven bed of down.' *Othello*, Act i. sc. 3.

Cf. also the King's speech in 2 *Henry IV*, iii. 1.

l. 90. *either.* Either properly means 'whichsoever of the two; whether one or the other.' Here it is incorrectly used of any one of five things.

l. 92. 'Johnson being asked by a young nobleman, what was become of the gallantry and military spirit of the old English nobility, he replied, "Why, my Lord, I'll tell you what is become of it; it is gone into the city to look for a fortune." '—*Life of Johnson*, ii. 126. See *post*, l. 395.

l. 95.
'What shocks one part will edify the rest,
Nor with one system can they all be blest:
The very best will variously incline,
And what rewards your virtue, punish mine.'
Pope, *Essay on Man*, iv. 141.

l. 98. *peculiar pain.* Pain which accompanies it alone. Compare Gray's *Ode on Vicissitude*, l. 41:—

'Still, where rosy pleasure leads,
See a kindred grief pursue.'

l. 100. Let us examine them in the countries that lie before us.

l. 101. *my proper cares. Proper*, in the sense of *one's own*; as in *Othello*, i. 3. 69, 'our proper son.'

l. 105. *Far to the right.* He must have seated himself with his face towards the east.

l. 108. Milton describes the border of Eden as:—

> 'A sylvan scene, and, as the ranks ascend
> Shade above shade, a woody theatre
> Of stateliest view.' *Paradise Lost*, iv. 140.

Cf. also the *Aeneid*, v. 288.

l. 113.
> 'Blossoms and fruits and flowers together rise,
> And the whole year in gay confusion lies.'
>   Addison, *Letter from Italy*.

l. 117. *sweets*. *Sweets*, which is properly used of the perfume, here stands for the flowers.

l. 118. *vernal lives*.
> 'Not to me returns
> Day, or the sweet approach of even or morn,
> Or sight of vernal bloom.' *Paradise Lost*, iii. 41.

l. 119. The flowers by their luxuriant and wanton growth show that the soil is natural to them. 'The planter's toil,' however, is as much needed in Italy as under 'the northern sky.' Gibbon, in the *Decline and Fall*, ch. xvii, examines into the causes of 'the amazing desolation' which rapidly spread over 'the fertile and happy province of Campania.'

l. 121. *sea-born gales*. *Sea-born*, that which is born of the sea, must be distinguished from *sea-borne*, that which is borne on the sea. *Gelid wings*. Cf. *Psalm* xviii. 10, 'the wings of the wind.' A gelid, i.e. an icy cold wind, would have destroyed the 'sweets,' and set the thinly-clad 'sons of Italy' shivering. Such a passage as this more properly belongs 'to the poetry of the period intervening between the publication of the *Paradise Lost* and the *Seasons*' (1667-1730); which, says Wordsworth, 'does not contain a single new image of external nature; and scarcely presents a familiar one from which it can be inferred that the eye of the poet had been steadily fixed upon his object, much less that his feelings had urged him to work upon it in the spirit of genuine imagination.'—Wordsworth's *Works*, ed. 1857, vi. 369.

l. 122. *winnow*. To *winnow* is properly *to separate by*

means of the wind; to part the grain from the chaff. The wind parts the fragrance from the flowers and scatters it as it moves along. Compare Gray's Ode, *On the Spring*, l. 9 :—

> 'Cool zephyrs thro' the clear blue sky
> Their gather'd fragrance fling.'

l. 123. *sense*, i.e. the five senses. Sensual bliss is the bliss that comes from any one of them. A curious parallel to these lines is found in *The Times*, by Churchill, published two or three months before *The Traveller* :—

> 'Italia, nurse of every softer art,
> Who, feigning to refine, unmans the heart,
> Who lays the realms of sense and virtue waste,
> Who mars whilst she pretends to mend our taste.'

Sense here means 'understanding, soundness of faculties, strength of natural reason.'

l. 125. *florid beauty.* Beauty bright in colour.

This passage is imitated by Heber in the lines :—

> 'What though the spicy breezes
> Blow soft o'er Ceylon's isle,
> Though every prospect pleases,
> And only man is vile.'

The previous stanza, which passes from Greenland to Africa, with its 'golden sand' and 'palmy plain' recalls lines 65–70. Compare Wordsworth's *Lines written in Early Spring* (*Works*, ed. 1857, iv. 198) :—

> 'To her fair works did Nature link
> The human soul that through me ran;
> And much it grieved my heart to think
> What man has made of man.'

l. 128. Compare a line of a passage in Denham, which, says Johnson, 'almost every writer for a century past has imitated' :—'Though deep, yet clear; though gentle, yet not dull.'—Johnson's *Works*, ed. 1825, vii. 62.

vain. 'The Italians,' writes Addison, 'affect always to appear sober and sedate; insomuch that one sometimes meets young men walking the streets with spectacles on their noses, that they may be thought to have impaired their sight by much study.'—*Works*, i. 373.

l. 133. *the date.* The poet is speaking of the Commonwealths of Italy which flourished in the Middle Ages, and had been slowly decaying.

l. 135. 'The new Street of Genoa,' writes Addison, 'is a double range of palaces from one end to the other, built with an excellent fancy, and fit for the greatest princes to inhabit.'—Addison's *Works*, ed. 1862, i. 362.

l. 136. Gibbon at the end of the *Decline and Fall* tells how at Rome in the fifteenth century 'prostrate obelisks were raised from the ground, and erected in the most conspicuous places.'

l. 137. *warm.* It is no merit in a painter to give unnaturally bright colours to his pictures. The line was perhaps suggested by one in Addison's *Letter from Italy*:—

'So warm with life his blended colours glow';

or by one in Dryden's *Lines to Sir Godfrey Kneller* :—

'So warm thy work, so glows the generous frame.'

l. 138. The quarry is likened to a woman giving birth to many children.

l. 140. 'The ordinary revolutions of war and government easily dry up the sources of that wealth which arises from commerce only. That which arises from the more solid improvements of agriculture is much more durable.'—*Wealth of Nations*, Bk. iii. ch. 4.

l. 142. *towns unmann'd.* Towns without inhabitants. Johnson does not give this meaning of the word.

lords without a slave. Churchill, in his lines on Italy, has :—

'The farce of greatness, without being great,
Pride without power, titles without estate.'

Poems, ed. 1766, ii. 267.

Goldsmith perhaps exaggerates the depopulation. Gibbon, describing a journey which he took in Italy in 1764, says :—
'I traversed a fruitful and populous country, which could alone disprove the paradox of Montesquieu, that modern Italy is a desert.'—*Misc. Works*, i. 197.

l. 144. *plethoric ill.* *Plethora* is 'an excessive fulness of blood,' due generally to overmuch food and drink. The poet implies that the nation had had an excess of opulence; which, though it seemed to give strength to the body politic, in the end left it weaker than before.

l. 147. *long-fall'n mind.* The mind that has been degraded for some generations.

l. 149. 'Happy country, where the pastoral age begins to revive! Where the wits even of Rome are united into a rural group of nymphs and swains under the appellation of modern Arcadians. Where, in the midst of porticos, processions, and cavalcades, abbés turned shepherds, and shepherdesses without sheep, indulge their innocent *divertimenti*.' —*Present State of Polite Learning*, ch. 4. Mr. Browning, in his *Up at a Villa—Down in the City*, shows that the modern Italian in this is like his forefathers.

'Noon strikes,—here sweeps the procession! our Lady borne
　smiling and smart,
With a pink gauze gown all spangles, and seven swords stuck in
　her heart!
Bang, whang, whang, goes the drum, *tootle-te-tootle* the fife;
No keeping one's haunches still : it's the greatest pleasure in life.'

l. 153. When Goldsmith was writing this poem, a friend (Sir Joshua Reynolds, it is believed), suddenly entering the room, found him engaged in teaching a favourite dog to beg. 'Occasionally he glanced his eye over his desk, and occasionally shook his finger at the unwilling pupil in order to make him retain his position; while on the page before him was written the couplet, with the ink of the second line still wet:—
　"By sports like these are all their cares beguiled,
　　The sports of children satisfy the child."'
The poet owned 'that the amusement in which he had been engaged had given birth to the idea.' Prior's *Goldsmith*. ii. 33.

l. 154.
　'Behold the child, by Nature's kindly law,
　Pleased with a rattle, tickled with a straw.'
　　　　　　Pope, *Essay on Man.* ii. 275

D

l. 155. Goldsmith, *Present State of Polite Learning*, ch. 4, describing the Italian Filosofi (Les philosophes) says:—
'Bred up all their lives in colleges, they have there learned to think in track, servilely to follow the leader of their sect, and only to adopt such opinions as their Universities, or the Inquisition, are pleased to allow.'

l. 156. *mans the soul.* See *ante* in note on l. 123, 'unmans the heart.'

l. 159. *domes.* Johnson defines *dome* in its primary meaning as 'a building, a house.' Compare in *The Vanity of Human Wishes*, l. 139:—

'O'er Bodley's dome his future labours spread.'

There is no dome, i.e. cupola, in the Bodleian Library.

l. 160. 'I am very glad,' wrote Horace Walpole in 1740, 'that I see Rome while it yet exists; before a great number of years are elapsed, I question whether it will be worth seeing. Between the ignorance and poverty of the present Romans, everything is neglected and falling to decay; the villas are entirely out of repair, and the palaces so ill kept, that half the pictures are spoiled by damp.'—*Letters*, i. 43.

l. 164. 'It was at Rome, on the 15th of October, 1764, as I sat musing amidst the ruins of the Capitol, while the bare-footed friars were singing vespers in the Temple of Jupiter, that the idea of writing the decline and fall of the city first started to my mind.'—Gibbon's *Misc. Works*, i. 198.

l. 166. 'La stérilité des terres rend les hommes industrieux, sobres, endurcis au travail, courageux, propres à la guerre; il faut bien qu'ils se procurent ce que le terrain leur refuse.'—Montesquieu, *Esprit des Lois*, xviii. 4.

l. 169. An allusion probably to Ovid, *Met.* iii. 110, 'seges clipeata virorum.' The product was but a base one—men who sold themselves as mercenary soldiers. With some reason did the French herald after Agincourt say:—

'—Many of our princes—woe the while!—
Lie drown'd and soak'd in mercenary blood.'
Henry V, act iv. sc. 7.

At the present time the product is more innocent—the hotel-waiters of Europe.

l. 171. There seems a trace of Johnson's hand in the next four lines.

l. 172.
> 'The flow'ry May, who from her green lap throws
> The yellow cowslip and the pale primrose.'
> Milton, *On May Morning.*

l. 176. *Redress the clime.* Remedy the hardships of the climate. Compare *The Deserted Village,* l. 422 :—
> 'Redress the rigours of th' inclement clime.'

l. 179.
> 'Where then, ah! where, shall poverty reside,
> To 'scape the pressure of contiguous pride?'
> *The Deserted Village,* l. 303.

rear its head. Compare Congreve's *Mourning Bride,* act ii. sc. 1 :—
> 'Whose ancient pillars rear their marble heads.'

l. 181. *No costly lord. Costly* here means *living at a great cost.*

deal. Distribute. Cf. Isaiah lviii. 7 :—'Is it not to deal thy bread to the hungry?'

l. 182. *his vegetable meal.* Compare in Goldsmith's *Hermit,* st. 13, 'his vegetable store.'

l. 184. The peasant adapts himself to his position as a tiller of the soil by limiting his desires. *Him* is put for *himself.*

l. 186. *Breasts.* In the first edition, 'breathes'; in the fourth, 'breasts'; in those published after Goldsmith's death, 'breathes.'

l. 187. *trolls.* Fishes for pike with a peculiar kind of rod.

finny deep. Pope has 'the fishy flood'; quoted in Johnson's *Dict.*

l. 188. *to the steep.* To the edge of the precipice.

l. 190. *savage.* The bear or wolf. Pope uses it of a boar, *Iliad,* xvii. 815 :—
> 'But if the savage turns his glaring eye,
> They howl aloof, and round the forest fly.'

l. 193. Compare the scenes described in Thomson's *Winter*, l. 311; Gray's *Elegy*, l. 21; and Burns's *Cotter's Saturday Night*, l. 19.

l. 196. *cleanly platter*. *Cleanly* is generally used of a person, or of a thing which makes cleanliness, not of a thing which is clean.

l. 197. Compare *The Deserted Village*, l. 155:—
'The broken soldier, kindly bade to stay,
Sat by his fire, and talk'd the night away.'

l. 198. Compare *Othello*, iv. 3:—'Give me my nightly wearing'; i. e. my clothes for the night.

l. 200. *the patriot passion*. Johnson defines *patriot* as 'one whose ruling passion is the love of his country.' Goldsmith here uses it as an adjective. *Patriotic* is not in Johnson's *Dict*.

l. 201. *mansion*. This is the second time (see l. 167) that the poet applies *mansion* to what he elsewhere calls a hut or a shed. To our ears the word has too big a sound.

l. 203. *conforms*. His soul with its modest desires wears, as it were, the same form as his modest house.

l. 211. These states must not be praised too highly. It is true that their wants are few, but their pleasures therefore are correspondingly few; for pleasure consists in redressing, i. e. relieving or gratifying, a want. As Johnson said, 'Every pleasure is of itself a good, unless counterbalanced by evil.'—*Life of Johnson*, iii. 327. On the other hand, he was fond of quoting 'the saying of the old philosopher, that he who wants least is most like the gods who want nothing.'—*Ib*. ii. 474, *n*. 3.

l. 216. *supplies*. Supplies the gratification of the desire.

l. 217. This passage may be illustrated by Milton's *Sonnet to Mr. Lawrence*:—
'What neat repast shall feast us, light and choice,
Of Attic taste, with wine, whence we may rise
To hear the lute well touch'd, or artful voice
Warble immortal notes and Tuscan air?'

l. 219. *those powers*. Poetry, music, eloquence, painting, and the like.

l. 221. Compare Browning's *Grammarian's Funeral*:—
'Our low life was the level's and the night's.'

l. 226.
'Some sunk to beasts find pleasure end in pain.'
Essay on Man, iv. 23.

Cf. Boswell's *Life of Johnson*, v. 156, n. 2.

l. 228. *low*. It is surprising that Goldsmith introduces this word, the fashionable use of which he ridiculed in *The Present State of Polite Learning*, ch. xi. 'By the power of one single monosyllable,' he writes, 'our critics have almost got the victory over humour amongst us. Does the poet paint the absurdity of the vulgar, then he is *low*; does he exaggerate the features of folly to render it more thoroughly ridiculous, he is then very *low*.' In *She Stoops to Conquer* one of the fellows in the ale-house says of Tony Lumpkin :— 'I loves to hear him sing, bekeays he never gives us nothing that's low.'

l. 229. Refinement is concerned with the pleasures of life. As it does not advance, so there is no improvement in morals.

l. 232. *Fall*. The verb is in the plural because there are two darts—that of love and that of friendship.

indurated. Hardened.

l. 236. *cultur'd*. Johnson (*Life of Gray*, 1781) says :— 'There has of late arisen a practice of giving to adjectives derived from substantives the termination of participles; such as the *cultured* plain; the daisied bank.'

l. 238. 'It is pretended that the sentiments of men become more delicate as the country approaches nearer to the sun; and that the taste of beauty and elegance receives proportional improvements in every latitude.'—Hume, *Essay, Of National Characters*.

l. 241. Compare *Deserted Village*, l. 5 :—

'Dear lovely bowers of innocence and ease,
Seats of my youth, when every sport could please,
How often have I loiter'd o'er thy green.'

France was not so gay as the poet represents her. Johnson in 1775 said :—'The great in France live very magnificently, but the rest very miserably.'—*Life of Johnson*,

ii. 402. Baretti, who travelled through it in 1760, denies that the French are cheerful. In Provence alone 'do you see with some sort of frequency the rustic assemblies roused up to cheerfulness by the *fifre* and the *tambourin*.'—Baretti's *Journey*, iv. 148. Rousseau wrote of them in 1777 :--'Cette nation qui se prétend si gaie montre peu cette gaîté dans ses jeux.'—*Les Rêveries, ixme promenade*.

l. 243. George Primrose, in the *Vicar of Wakefield*, ch. 20, describing his wanderings says :—' I passed [as a musician] among the harmless peasants of Flanders, and among such of the French as were poor enough to be very merry ; for I ever found them sprightly in proportion to their wants. Whenever I approached a peasant's house towards nightfall, I played one of my most merry tunes, and that procured me not only a lodging but subsistence for the next day.' Goldsmith, in *The Present State of Polite Learning*, ch. 6, tells how Holberg, ' without money, recommendations, or friends, undertook to set out upon his travels, and make the tour of Europe on foot. A good voice and a trifling skill in music were the only finances he had to support an undertaking so extensive ; so he travelled by day, and at night sung at the doors of peasants' houses to get himself a lodging.'

l. 244. *tuneless*. Unharmonious, unmusical. Johnson quotes from Spenser :—

'When in hand my tuneless harp I take.'

l. 253. *gestic*. 'Johnson neglected or omitted this word in his *Dictionary*; though he might have learnt what Goldsmith really meant by it. The context seems to connect it with *gesture* and *gesticulate*.' Latham's *Dict*. The first edition of Johnson's *Dictionary* came out nearly ten years before *The Traveller* ; but to the 4th edition he made, in 1773, many additions. Scott has borrowed the word in *Peveril of the Peak*, ch. 30, as Professor Hales points out.

l. 254. *frisk'd*. Compare Gray's *Progress of Poesy*, l. 31 :—

'Frisking light in frolic measures.'

l. 256. *idly busy*. 'Life's idle business.'—Pope, *Elegy to an Unfortunate Lady*.

l. 258. The disposition of the mind, in the daily intercourse of men, is formed by a regard to reputation.

l. 260. Johnson, in his *London*, l. 69, says of 'the supple Gaul':—

> 'Still to his int'rest true, where'er he goes,
> Wit, brav'ry, worth, his lavish tongue bestows;
> In ev'ry face a thousand graces shine,
> From ev'ry tongue flows harmony divine.'

l. 264. *an avarice of praise.* Compare, 'laudumque immensa cupido,' *Aeneid*, vi. 823; 'praeter laudem nullius avaris,' *Ars Poetica*, l. 324, and the passage in *Henry V*, Act iv. sc. 3, where the King says:—

> 'By Jove, I am not covetous for gold,
> . . . . . .
> But if it be a sin to covet honour,' &c.

l. 265. *they give to get esteem.* Compare, 'Sunt qui alios laudent laudentur ut ipsi.'

l. 269. *warmly sought.* Eagerly, or ardently sought.

l. 273-4. There is a Johnsonian ring about this couplet.

l. 276. Robe is a gown of state, a dress of dignity, while frieze is a coarse warm cloth. The lace should have been textures of thread with gold or silver, but it is of copper.

l. 277. The food and drink which should have been the cheer at each day's meals are stinted by a despicable pride.

l. 281. On Italy, Switzerland, and France he had looked down from his 'crag among the Alps,' but to Holland his fancy only can extend.

l. 284. Cf. Dryden's *Annus Mirabilis*, st. 164:—

> 'Then we upon our globe's last verge shall go,
> And view the ocean leaning on the sky.'

This stanza Johnson describes as an 'absurdity, of which perhaps Dryden was not conscious.' Johnson's *Works*, ed. 1825, vii. 341. As at high water the ocean rises above Holland—at least above a part of it –it may be said to lean against the land.

l. 286. *rampire.* Rampart.

artificial pride. The bank raised by art rises proudly above the sea.

l. 287. *diligently slow.* The bulwark is the slowly produced result of diligent labour.

l. 290. Goldsmith, in his *Animated Nature*, ed. 1779, i. 276, says: 'The whole Republic of Holland seems to be a conquest upon the sea, and in a manner rescued from its bosom. The surface of the earth in 'his country is below the level of the bed of the sea; and remember, upon approaching the coast, to have looked down upon it from the sea, as into a valley.'

Usurps the shore. Compare

'trade's unfeeling train
Usurp the land.'   *The Deserted Village*, l. 63.

l. 292. *amphibious world.* Amphibious, because with its vales and its canals it partakes of two natures, land and water.

l. 294. *the gliding sail.* Sir W. Temple in 1673 describes 'the infinity of sails that are seen everywhere coursing up and down upon the canals.'—Temple's *Works*, ed. 1757, i. 149.

l. 297. 'The flatness of their land forces them to infinite charge in the continual fences and repairs of their banks to oppose the sea; which employs yearly more men than all the corn of the Province of Holland could maintain.'—*Ib.* p. 151. Their 'strange assiduity and constant application of their minds, with that perpetual study and labour upon anything they take in hand,' is perhaps due, Temple thinks, to 'the dulness of their air.'—*Ib.* p. 161.

l. 302. See the Dedication to *The Deserted Village* for Goldsmith's attack on luxury; and Boswell's *Johnson*, ii. 217, for a discussion with Johnson on this subject, in which he maintains that a pickle-shop is harmful because luxurious.

l. 305. Temple and Arbuthnot both give them a better character. 'They make use of their skill and their wit,' writes Temple, 'to take advantage of other men's ignorance and folly; are great exacters, where the law is in their own hands: in other points, where they deal with men that understand like themselves, and are under the reach of justice and laws, they are the plainest and best dealers in the world.'—Temple's *Works*, i. 154. Arbuthnot, in his *History of John Bull*, writes in 1712:—'Nic. Frog [the Dutchman] was cunning and sly, quite the reverse of John in many particulars; covetous, frugal; minded domestic affairs; would pinch his belly to ·ve his pocket; never lost a farthing by careless servants or bad debtors.... Yet it must be owned that Nic. was a fair dealer, and in that way acquired immense riches.'—Swift's *Works*, ed. 1803, xxiii. 161.

l. 307. 'This stomachful people, who could not endure the least exercise of arbitrary power or impositions, or the sight of any foreign troops, under the Spanish government, have since been inured to all of them, in the highest degree, under their own popular magistrates; bridled with hard laws, terrified with severe executions, environed with foreign forces; and oppressed with the most cruel hardship and variety of taxes that was ever known under any government.' —Temple's *Works*, i. 137. 'In Holland, Switzerland, and Genoa, new laws are not frequently enacted, but the old ones are observed with unremitting severity. In such republics, therefore, the people are slaves to laws of their own making.' —*Citizen of the World*, Letter 49. 'In Asia I find the Dutch the great Lords of all the Indian seas; in Europe the timid inhabitants of a paltry state. No longer the sons of freedom, but of avarice; no longer assertors of their rights by courage, but by negotiations; fawning on those who insult them, and crouching under the rod of every neighbouring power.'—*Ib.* Letter 55. 'The Dutch merchants [in Japan] have raised my dislike to Europe in general; by them I learn how low avarice can degrade human nature; how many indignities an European will suffer for gain.'—*Ib.* Letter 117. In a passage which appears only in the first edition of *The Present State of Polite Learning*, Goldsmith, writing about a guinea, says:—'A native of Madagascar prefers to it a glass bead; a native of Holland prefers it to everything else.'—Goldsmith's *Works*, ed. 1854, i. 417.

l. 309. Goldsmith uses the same words of the Persians :—
'A nation famous for setting the world an example of freedom is now become a land of tyrants and a den of slaves.' —*Citizen of the World*, Letter 34. Johnson had described Jamaica as 'a place of great wealth and dreadful wickedness. a den of tyrants and a dungeon of slaves.'—*Works*, vi. 130. Yet Goldsmith, writing about Holland from Leyden, had said: 'No misery is to be seen here; every one is usefully employed.'—Prior's *Goldsmith*, i. 163. In *The Bee*, No. 5, he says: 'The best and the most useful laws I have ever seen are generally practised in Holland.'

l. 310. *dishonourable graves.*

'Peep about
To find ourselves dishonourable graves.'
Julius Caesar, i. 2. 137.

l. 312. The lakes, lying low and being sheltered by the sea-banks, would not catch the wind.

l. 313. Caesar writes of the Belgic Nervii :—'Nullum aditum esse ad eos mercatoribus; nihil pati vini reliquarumque rerum ad luxuriam pertinentium inferri, quod iis rebus relanguescere animos et remitti virtutem existimarent: esse homines feros magnaeque virtutis, increpitare atque incusare reliquos Belgas, qui se populo Romano dedidissent patriamque virtutem projecissent.'—*De Bell. Gall.* ii. 15. Belgium was adopted as the diplomatic name of the Netherlands in the sixteenth century.

l. 315. Compare l. 327.

l. 316. This weak line is introduced for the sake of the transition from one part of the poem to another.

l. 317. *her wing.* Johnson, criticising the Ode of a lank bony bard, said '"Here is an error, Sir; you have made Genius feminine." "Palpable, Sir," cried the enthusiast, "I know it. But (in a lower tone) it was to pay a compliment to the Duchess of Devonshire, with which her Grace was pleased. She is walking across Coxheath, in the military uniform, and I suppose her to be the Genius of Britain." JOHNSON. "Sir, you are giving a reason for it; but that will not make it right. You may have a reason why two and

two should make five : but they will still make but four."'
Life of Johnson, iii. 374.

l. 319. *lawns.* Johnson defines *lawn* as 'an open space between woods.' Pope writes of 'the flow'ry lawn,' *Essay on Man*, iii. 30. This shows the change in meaning; for a modern lawn is never suffered to be flowery. Goldsmith addresses Auburn as—

'Sweet smiling village. loveliest of the lawn.'
The Deserted Village, l. 35.

See also *ib.* l. 65.

Arcadian pride. Arcadia was looked upon as the home of pastoral poetry.

'Of famous Arcady ye are.' Milton, *Arcades*, l. 28.

'Let old Arcadia boast her ample plain.'
Pope, *Windsor Forest*, l. 159.

l. 320. *famed Hydaspes.*
' Quae loca fabulosus
Lambit Hydaspes.' Horace, i. *Odes* xxii. 7.

'The springs
Of Ganges or Hydaspes, Indian streams.'
Paradise Lost, iii. 435.

l. 321. Compare in John of Gaunt's noble praise of England—
'This other Eden, demi-paradise.'
Richard II, act ii. sc. 1. l. 42.

l. 324. It is the Englishman, the owner or master of England, who is full of extremes. Compare what Pope says of Nature :—

'Obvious her goods, in no extreme they dwell.'
Essay on Man, iv. 31.

l. 325. 'We talked of Goldsmith's *Traveller*, of which Dr. Johnson spoke highly ; and while I was helping him on with his great-coat, he repeated from it the character of the British nation, which he did with such energy that the tear started into his eye.'—*Life of Johnson*, v. 344. Little more than seven years before these lines were written, Lord

Chesterfield, a statesman of great experience, wrote:—
'Whoever is in or whoever is out, I am sure we are undone both at home and abroad; at home, by our increasing debt and expenses; abroad, by our ill-luck and incapacity. . . . The French are masters to do what they please in America. We are no longer a nation. I never yet saw so dreadful a prospect.'—Chesterfield, *Misc. Works*, iv. 198. The great conquests made when Pitt (the Earl of Chatham) was war minister had intervened. Macaulay, writing of the close of the reign of George II, says:—' Pitt was the first Englishman of his time; and he had made England the first country in the world . . . The nation was drunk with joy and pride.'—Macaulay's *Essays*, ed. 1874, ii. 195.

l. 327. 'Pride seems the source not only of the national vices of Englishmen, but of their national virtues also.'—*Citizen of the World*, Letter iv.

l. 328. 'Romanos rerum dominos.'—*Aeneid*, i. 282.

l. 332. *True to imagin'd right.* True to whatever they imagine to be their right.

l. 333. 'The lowest mechanic looks upon it as his duty to be a watchful guardian of his country's freedom, and often uses a language that might seem haughty, even in the mouth of the great Emperor who traces his ancestry to the moon.'—*Citizen of the World*, Letter iv. In this Letter Goldsmith describes the alarm of a prisoner for debt, lest the French should come over and take away our liberty. A porter is introduced, who abuses them as 'slaves, fit only to carry burdens'; while a soldier exclaims, as he drinks a pot of beer:

'May the Devil sink me into flames, if the French should come over here but our religion would be utterly undone.'

l. 340. 'In some countries it is almost as easy to get a good estate as a good acquaintance. In England, particularly, acquaintance is of almost as slow growth as an oak; so that the age of man scarce suffices to bring it to any perfection.' —Fielding's *Amelia*, Bk. iii. ch. 8. '"Sir,'" said Johnson, "two men of any other nation who are shown into a room together, at a house where they are both visitors, will immediately find some conversation. But two Englishmen will probably go each to a different window, and remain in obstinate silence. Sir, we as yet do not enough understand the common rights of humanity." '—*Life of Johnson*, iv. 191.

l. 341. *lordlings*. Each Englishman plays the part of a little lord, depending only on himself. Compare the proud saying, 'An Englishman's house is his castle.'

l. 343. In the first edition—
  'See, though by circling deeps together held.'

'The bonds of nature' are the seas, which, though they hold Britons together, are but a feeble bond of union.

l. 345. *imprison'd factions.* Imprison'd in an island.

l. 346. Perhaps this refers to Jacobite invasions.

l. 353. Johnson said, 'No man now has the same authority which his father had—except a gaoler. No master has it over his servants; it is diminished in our colleges; nay, in our grammar schools . . . There is a general relaxation of reverence.'—*Life of Johnson*, iii. 262.

l. 354.
 'This mournful truth is ev'rywhere confess'd,
 Slow rises worth by poverty depress'd;
 But here more slow, where all are slaves to gold,
 Where looks are merchandise, and smiles are sold.'
       Johnson, *London*, l. 120.

l. 356. *the nurse of arms.* Compare Richard II :—
 'This nurse, this teeming womb of royal Kings,
 Fear'd by their breed.' *Richard II*, Act ii. 1. 51.

l. 358. *wrote*, used for 'written,' a common usage last century.

l. 360.
 'Yet come it will, the day decreed by fates;
 (How my heart trembles while my tongue relates!
 The day when thou, imperial Troy, must bend,
 And see thy warriors fall, thy glories end.'
      Pope, *Homer's Iliad*, vi. 570.

Cf. too the end of Pope's *Dunciad* :—
 'Nor public flame, nor private dares to shine:
 Nor human spark is left, nor glimpse divine.'

l. 361. 'Basil Montagu related that Dr. Scott [afterwards Lord Stowell] informed him that he waited on Goldsmith to make a proposal,' on the part of Lord North [the Prime Minister] that he should write on behalf of the Ministry. He was offered any compensation he might desire. He said he could earn from the booksellers as much as his necessities required, and he would rather live without being obliged to any one. Scott told this as a proof of Goldsmith's ignorance of the world.'—*Diary of H. C. Robinson*, ii. 129.

l. 363. In the first edition—

'Perish the wish ; for inly satisfied,
Above their pomps I hold my ragged pride.'

'Ragged pride' the poet perhaps suppressed because it told too much of 'the sordid past.' See Forster's *Goldsmith*, i. 375. Yet once 'in a circle of good company, he began with—"When I lived among the beggars in Axe Lane."'—*Ib.* p. 76 *n.*

In *The Present State of Polite Learning*, ch. 13, he writes:—'A man who is whirled through Europe in a postchaise, and the pilgrim who walks the grand tour on foot, will form very different conclusions.' To this in the first edition was added in a foot-note—'Haud inexpertus loquor.' In the second edition, which he lived to revise, but not perhaps to publish, this note does not appear.

l. 370. That the flower of Freedom may bloom uninjured by sudden changes in the climate, its luxuriance must be restrained.

l. 372. 'Thus let the wiser make the rest obey.'—*Essay on Man*, iii. 196.

l. 374. The highest aim of freedom is to lay on each class in the state, and on each man in the class, his fair share of public burdens.

l. 376. *all below.* The poet would have held that disproportion in any of the orders below the highest would ruin all above as well as all below. He is upholding here what Johnson calls 'the series of civil subordination' (*Life of Johnson*, ii. 244), without which 'order cannot be had' (*ib.* iii. 383). Thomson makes the Goddess of Liberty tell of

l. 378.
> 'The calm gradations of art-nursing peace,
> And matchless Orders, the deep basis still
> On which ascends my British reign.' *Liberty*, iv. 687.
>
> 'Order is heav'n's first law; and this confest,
> Some are, and must be, greater than the rest.'
> *Essay on Man*, iv. 49.

l. 382. Fifteen years later the House of Commons passed a resolution 'that the influence of the Crown has increased, is increasing, and ought to be diminished.'—*Life of Johnson*, iv. 220.

l. 383. 'As the Roman senators by slow and imperceptible degrees became masters of the people, yet still flattered them with a show of freedom, while themselves only were free; so is it possible for a body of men, while they stand up for privileges, to grow into an exuberance of power themselves, and the public become actually dependent, while some of its individuals only governed.'—*Citizen of the World*, Letter 49. By 'a body of men' Parliament is meant.

l. 385. Much of the legislation of the Whig Government in the time of George II was unpopular from the restraints imposed in many ways on social liberty. Goldsmith, in *The Citizen of the World*, No. 71, makes a foolish attack on Lord Chancellor Hardwicke's Marriage Act (1753), by which much was done to put an end to clandestine marriages. (See Smollett's *England*, ed. 1800, iii. 349.) In the same year the act for licensing ale-houses was carried; described by Smollett as 'an Act which empowered the Justices of Peace to tyrannise over their fellow subjects.'—*Ib.* p. 346. In London, at all events, they were often unfit to exercise this power; for 'many of them were men of profligate lives, needy, mean, ignorant, and rapacious, and often acted from the most scandalous principles of selfish avarice.' *Ib.* p. 331. By 'each wanton judge' is perhaps meant the Lord Chancellor of the Whig Government for the time being, who was responsible for the new statutes which were made by Parliament.

l. 386. Dr. Primrose describes Holland, Genoa, and Venice

as places 'where the laws govern the poor, and the rich govern the law.'—*Vicar of Wakefield*, ch. 19.

l. 387. Goldsmith perhaps in this couplet mixes up the recent conquests in America and India. Johnson described the war with the French in Canada 'as the quarrel of two robbers for the spoils of a passenger.'—*Life of Johnson*, ii. 479. From India were returning every year the 'Nabobs,' —men who by extortion had accumulated vast fortunes. The slaves they purchased at home were parliamentary voters. See *ib.* v. 106, where Boswell regrets 'that a Nabob now would carry an election from men of family.' Clive bought seats for his dependents. 'After the election of 1761, he found himself in the House of Commons at the head of a body of dependents whose support must have been important to any administration.'—Macaulay's *Essays*, ed. 1874, iii. 136.

l. 390. Compare

'Bare the mean heart that lurks beneath a star.'

Pope, *Sat.* i. 108;

and

'envious malice of thy swelling heart.'

1 *Henry VI*, Act iii. sc. 1.

l. 392. Hume, in his *Essay on the British Government*, says :—'It is well known that every government must come to a period, and that death is unavoidable to the political, as well as to the animal body.' He goes on to say that if a republic is established, 'we shall suffer all the tyranny of a faction subdivided into new factions'; and concludes :—'Absolute monarchy, therefore, is the easiest death, the true *euthanasia* of the British Constitution.'—*Works*, ed. 1770, i. 53. Lord Bolingbroke, in his *Patriot King*, had held up a virtuous king, possessed of absolute power, as a nearly divine spectacle. Bolingbroke's *Works*, ed. 1809, iv. 332. Dr. Primrose says :—'I am then for, and would die for, monarchy, sacred monarchy; for if there be anything sacred amongst men, it must be the anointed Sovereign of his people, and every diminution of his power in war or in peace is an infringement upon the real liberties of the subject.

The sounds of liberty, patriotism, and Britons have already done *much*; it is to be hoped that the true sons of freedom will prevent their ever doing more.'—*Vicar of Wakefield*, ch. 19. His son, George, summing up the results of his observations on his travels, says:—' I found that monarchy was the best government for the poor to live in, and commonwealths for the rich.'—*Ib.* ch. 20.

l. 395. *in its source.* 'The king is the fountain of honour.' —Bacon's *Essay, Of a King.*

l. 396. Dr. Primrose points out how in commercial states 'the learned are held unqualified to serve their country as counsellors merely from a defect of opulence, and wealth is thus made the object of a wise man's ambition . . . . the possessor of accumulated wealth, when furnished with the necessaries and pleasures of life, has no other method to employ the superfluity of his fortune but in purchasing power. That is, differently speaking, in making dependants, by purchasing the liberty of the needy or the venal . . . . In such a state all that the middle order has left, is to preserve the prerogative and privileges of the one principal governor with the most sacred circumspection. For he divides the power of the rich, and calls off the great from falling with tenfold weight on the middle order placed beneath them.' —*Vicar of Wakefield*, ch. 19. See *ante* l. 92.

l. 397. Compare *Deserted Village*, l. 51 : --

> 'Ill fares the land, to hastening ills a prey,
> Where wealth accumulates, and men decay;
> Princes and lords may flourish, or may fade;
> A breath can make them, as a breath has made;
> But a bold peasantry, their country's pride,
> When once destroy'd can never be supplied.'

The whole of that poem is but a beautiful expansion of the passage in the text. Johnson, in his *London*, published in 1738, had looked upon emigration as an escape :—

> 'Has Heaven reserv'd in pity to the poor,
> No pathless waste, or undiscover'd shore?

. . . .

E

'Quick let us rise, the happy seats explore.
And bear oppression's insolence no more.'

In his *Life of Savage* (1744) he looks upon 'the flight of every honest man as a loss to the community.'—*Life of Johnson*, i. 130, n. 2. In 1773 'he regretted emigration as hurtful to human happiness.'—*Ib.* v. 27. The Highlanders were emigrating in large numbers. In 1778 Burke said:—'We hear prodigious complaints at present of emigration.'—*Ib.* iii. 231. In the *Gentleman's Magazine* for 1773, p. 467, it is stated that 'the emigrations from the north of Ireland have at last roused the nobility and gentry of that country to enter into an association to discourage all monopolisers of land, to portion out their estates in smaller parcels, and to let those parcels at such moderate rents as will establish an interest to the tenant in the leases, and enable them to live something like the independent yeomanry of this kingdom.'

l. 398. *useless ore.* Compare *Deserted Village*, l. 269:—

'Proud swells the tide with loads of freighted ore.'

l. 402. Goldsmith, in his Dedication of the *Deserted Village* to Reynolds, says:—'I know you will object (and indeed several of our best and wisest friends concur in the opinion) that the depopulation it [the poem] deplores is nowhere to be seen.' He maintains that it does exist. There was no census, so that the poet's imagination had free play. A Bill to establish 'an Annual Register of the People' was carried through the House of Commons in 1753; but it was thrown out in the Lords 'as a scheme of very dangerous tendency.' Smollett's *Hist. of Eng.*, ed. 1800, iii. 355. The first census in Great Britain was taken in 1801; in Ireland, in 1813. *Census* is not in Johnson's *Dict.* At the present time it is not depopulation, but population, that is looked upon as 'stern.'

l. 405. Compare *Deserted Village*, lines 341–384.

l. 411. Fort Oswego, close to Lake Ontario, was taken by the French in 1756. In a plan of it in the *Gentleman's Magazine* for 1757 (p. 79), a large swamp is marked. In the general conquest of Canada, in 1759, it came again into the power of the English.

l. 412. Fort Niagara surrendered to the English on July 25, 1759.—*Gentleman's Magazine*, 1759, p. 437. Goldsmith, in throwing the accent on the last syllable but one, gives the word its true quantity. Forty-six years later it had lost its noble sound :—

'Mixt with the roaring of Niagara's fall,'

writes Mrs. Barbauld in her *Eighteen Hundred and Eleven*.

l. 414. *tangled forests*. Compare 'matted woods,' *Deserted Village*, l. 349.

l. 415.

'Where crouching tigers wait their hapless prey,
And savage men more murderous still than they;
While oft in whirls the mad tornado flies.' *Ib.* l. 355.

l. 417. *giddy tempest*. Either the whirling tempest, or the tempest which causes giddiness.

l. 418. *distressful yells*. If the yells are the cries of the savages, *distressful* means *causing distress* ; if of the exiles, *full of distress*.

l. 419. *pensive exile*. *Pensive*, defined by Johnson as 'sorrowfully thoughtful ; mournfully serious,' seems a strange epithet applied to a man in the midst of such horrors.

l. 420. This line was supplied by Johnson, as well as lines 429-434, and 437-8. *Life of Johnson*, ii. 6.

l. 421. *casts a long look*. Johnson, quoting from Sir Philip Sidney, 'casting a long look that way'; and from Dryden,

'casts out
Many a long look for succour'

interprets *long*, 'longing; desirous ; or perhaps, long-continued ; from the disposition to continue looking at anything desired.'

l. 422. His bosom sympathises with the poet's in the feelings expressed in the whole poem, and summed up in the next four lines. He left England in the search for bliss ; and now he looks back to her with longing.

l. 427. See *ante*, note on l. 50 of the Dedication.

l. 429. Johnson wrote to Baretti on Dec. 21, 1762 :—' The good or ill success of battles and embassies extends itself to a very small part of domestic life; we all have good and evil, which we feel more sensibly than our petty part of public miscarriage or prosperity.'—*Life of Johnson*, i. 381. In *The Rambler*, No. 68, he says:—'Very few are involved in great events, or have their thread of life entwisted with the chain of causes on which nations or armies are suspended .... To be happy at home is the ultimate result of all ambition, the end to which every enterprise and labour tends, and of which every desire prompts the prosecution.'

l. 431.

'Caelum, non animum, mutant qui trans mare currunt.'
Horace, 1 *Epis*. xi. 27.

'The mind is its own place, and in itself
Can make a heaven of hell, a hell of heaven.'
Paradise Lost, i. 254.

'If then to all men happiness was meant,
God in externals could not place content.'
Essay on Man, iv. 65.

l. 432. 'It is,' said Johnson, 'by studying little things that we attain the great art of having as little misery and as much happiness as possible.'—*Life of Johnson*, i. 433.

l. 435. *agonising wheel*. To *agonise* is properly 'to feel agonies.' See Pope, *Essay on Man*, i. 198:—

'To smart and agonise at every pore';

and Dryden, *The Hind and the Panther*, iii. 287:—

'Oh, sharp convulsive pangs of agonising pride.'

l. 436. *Luke's iron crown*. Two brothers, George and Luke Dosa, headed a rebellion in Hungary in 1514. 'George, not Luke, was punished by his head being encircled with a red-hot iron crown: "corona candescente ferrea coronatur."'—*Life of Johnson*, ii. 7, and Forster's *Goldsmith*, i. 370. Damiens, a madman, had, in 1757, made an attempt on the life of the King of France. For this he was put to death with the most infernal cruelties that the science of man could devise. Goldsmith, it is reported, said that by 'the bed of steel' he meant the rack. But Mr. Austin

Dobson quotes from Smollett's *History of England*, bk. iii.
7. 25: 'Being conducted to the conciergerie, an *iron bed*,
which likewise served for a chair, was prepared for him;
and to this he was fastened with chains.' Compare 'steel
couch of war,' quoted in note on l. 86.

    l. 437. *known*. This is a feeble word when used of such
dreadful torments.

THE END.

THE CLARENDON ENGLISH CLASSICS.

"No more alluring guides could be imagined into the pleasure garden of English Literature."—*Academy.*

VOLUMES ALREADY PUBLISHED.

MILTON.
   Paradise Lost, Book I. Edited by H. C. BEECHING, B.A. . . . . 3s. 6d.

BUNYAN.
   The Pilgrim's Progress, Grace Abounding, Relation of the Imprisonment of Mr. John Bunyan. Edited by E. VENABLES, M.A. . . . . 6s.

ADDISON.
   Selections from Papers in the Spectator. Edited by T. ARNOLD, M.A. . . . . 6s.

STEELE.
   Selections from the Tatler, Spectator, and Guardian. Edited by AUSTIN DOBSON . . . . 7s. 6d.

GOLDSMITH.
   Selected Poems. Edited by AUSTIN DOBSON . 4s. 6d.

JOHNSON.
   Rasselas. Edited by G. BIRKBECK HILL, D.C.L. 4s. 6d.

GRAY.
   Selected Poems. Edited by EDMUND GOSSE, M.A. 3s.

BYRON.
   Childe Harold. Edited by H. F. TOZER, M.A. 5s.

SCOTT.
   Lay of the Last Minstrel. Edited by W. MINTO, M.A. 3s. 6d.

☞ The CLARENDON ENGLISH CLASSICS are bound in ornamental parchment, with uncut edges and gilt top.

LONDON: HENRY FROWDE, AMEN CORNER, E.C.

MASTERPIECES
OF
THE FRENCH DRAMA.

EDITED

WITH PROLEGOMENA AND NOTES
FOR ENGLISH READERS.

———•———

1. *CORNEILLE.*
    Horace. Edited by GEORGE SAINTSBURY, M.A.
2. *MOLIÈRE.*
    Les Précieuses Ridicules. Edited by ANDREW LANG, M.A.
3. *RACINE.*
    Esther. Edited by GEORGE SAINTSBURY, M.A.
4. *VOLTAIRE.*
    Mérope. Edited by GEORGE SAINTSBURY, M.A.
5. *BEAUMARCHAIS.*
    Le Barbier de Séville. Edited by AUSTIN DOBSON.
6. *ALFRED DE MUSSET.*
    On ne badine pas avec l'Amour and *Fantasio.* By WALTER HERRIES POLLOCK.

Six vols. together in case, and bound in Imitation Parchment, suitable for Prizes, price 12s. 6d.

———

' The result is decidedly taking.'—*Athenæum.*

' For a studious youth we can scarcely conceive a finer and more appropriate book-gift.'—*Publisher's Circular*, Christmas, 1886.

' The prettiest present imaginable.'—*Bookseller.*

April, 1888.

The Clarendon Press, Oxford,
LIST OF SCHOOL BOOKS,
PUBLISHED FOR THE UNIVERSITY BY
HENRY FROWDE,
AT THE OXFORD UNIVERSITY PRESS WAREHOUSE,
AMEN CORNER, LONDON.

** *All Books are bound in Cloth, unless otherwise described.*

LATIN.

Allen. *An Elementary Latin Grammar.* By J. BARROW ALLEN, M.A.
Fifty-seventh Thousand . . . . . . Extra fcap. 8vo. 2s. 6d.
Allen. *Rudimenta Latina.* By the same Author. Extra fcap. 8vo. 2s.
Allen. *A First Latin Exercise Book.* By the same Author. *Fourth Edition.* . . . . Extra fcap. 8vo. 2s. 6d.
Allen. *A Second Latin Exercise Book.* By the same Author.
Extra fcap. 8vo. 3s. 6d.
[*A Key to First and Second Latin Exercise Books nearly ready.*]
Jerram. *Anglice Reddenda; or Extracts, Latin and Greek, for Unseen Translation.* By C. S. JERRAM, M.A. *Fourth Edition.*
Extra fcap. 8vo. 2s. 6d.
Jerram. *Anglice Reddenda.* SECOND SERIES. By C. S. JERRAM, M.A.
Extra fcap. 8vo. 3s.
Jerram. *Reddenda Minora; or, Easy Passages, Latin and Greek, for Unseen Translation.* For the use of Lower Forms. Composed and selected by C. S. JERRAM, M.A. . . . . . . Extra fcap. 8vo. 1s. 6d.
Lee-Warner. *Hints and Helps for Latin Elegiacs.*
Extra fcap. 8vo. 3s. 6d.
[*A Key is provided: for Teachers only.*]
Lewis and Short. *A Latin Dictionary,* founded on Andrews' Edition of Freund's Latin Dictionary. By CHARLTON T. LEWIS, Ph.D., and CHARLES SHORT, LL.D. . . . . 4to. 25s.
Nunns. *First Latin Reader.* By T. J. NUNNS, M.A. *Third Edition.*
Extra fcap. 8vo. 2s.
Papillon. *A Manual of Comparative Philology* as applied to the Illustration of Greek and Latin Inflections. By T. L. PAPILLON, M.A. *Third Edition.*
Crown 8vo. 6s.
Ramsay. *Exercises in Latin Prose Composition.* With Introduction, Notes, and Passages of graduated difficulty for Translation into Latin. By G. G. RAMSAY, M.A., Professor of Humanity, Glasgow. *Second Edition.*
Extra fcap. 8vo. 4s. 6d.
Sargent. *Passages for Translation into Latin.* By J. Y. SARGENT, M.A. *Seventh Edition.* . . . . . . Extra fcap. 8vo. 2s. 6d.
[*A key to this Edition is provided: for Teachers only.*]

Caesar. *The Commentaries* (for Schools). With Notes and Maps. By CHARLES E. MOBERLY, M.A.
    Part I. *The Gallic War. Second Edition.* . . Extra fcap. 8vo. 4s. 6d.
    Part II. *The Civil War.* . . . . . Extra fcap. 8vo. 3s. 6d.
    The Civil War. Book I. *Second Edition.* . . Extra fcap. 8vo. 2s.

Catulli Veronensis *Carmina Selecta*, secundum recognitionem ROBINSON ELLIS, A.M. . . . . . . Extra fcap. 8vo. 3s. 6d.

Cicero. *Selection of interesting and descriptive passages.* With Notes. By HENRY WALFORD, M.A. In three Parts. *Third Edition.*
                                                     Extra fcap. 8vo. 4s. 6d.
    Part I. *Anecdotes from Grecian and Roman History.* . limp, 1s. 6d.
    Part II. *Omens and Dreams; Beauties of Nature.* . . limp, 1s. 6d.
    Part III. *Rome's Rule of her Provinces.* . . . . limp, 1s. 6d.

Cicero. *De Senectute.* With Introduction and Notes. By LEONARD HUXLEY, B.A. *In one or two Parts* . . . Extra fcap. 8vo. 2s.

Cicero. *Pro Cluentio.* With Introduction and Notes. By W. RAMSAY, M.A. Edited by G. G. RAMSAY, M.A. *Second Edition.* Extra fcap. 8vo. 3s. 6d.

Cicero. *Selected Letters* (for Schools). With Notes. By the late C. E. PRICHARD, M.A., and E. R. BERNARD, M.A. *Second Edition.*
                                                     Extra fcap. 8vo. 3s.

Cicero. *Select Orations* (for Schools). *First Action against Verres; Oration concerning the command of Gnaeus Pompeius; Oration on behalf of Archias; Ninth Philippic Oration.* With Introduction and Notes. By J. R. KING, M.A. *Second Edition.* . . . . Extra fcap. 8vo. 2s. 6d.

Cicero. *In Q. Caecilium Divinatio* and *In C. Verrem Actio Prima.* With Introduction and Notes. By J. R. KING, M.A.
                                                 Extra fcap. 8vo. limp, 1s. 6d.

Cicero. *Speeches against Catilina.* With Introduction and Notes. By E. A. UPCOTT, M.A. *In one or two Parts.* . . Extra fcap. 8vo. 2s. 6d.

Cicero. *Philippic Orations.* With Notes, &c. by J. R. KING, M.A. *Second Edition.* . . . . 8vo. 10s. 6d.

Cicero. *Select Letters.* With English Introductions, Notes, and Appendices. By ALBERT WATSON, M.A. *Third Edition.* . . . 8vo. 18s.

Cicero. *Select Letters.* Text. By the same Editor. *Second Edition.*
                                                    Extra fcap. 8vo. 4s.

Cornelius Nepos. With Notes. By OSCAR BROWNING, M.A.
                                                 Extra fcap. 8vo. 2s. 6d.

Horace. With a Commentary. Volume I. *The Odes Carmen Seculare,* and *Epodes.* By EDWARD C. WICKHAM, M.A., Head Master of Wellington College. *New Edition. In one or two Parts.* Extra fcap. 8vo. 6s.

Horace. *Selected Odes.* With Notes for the use of a Fifth Form. By E. C. WICKHAM, M.A. *In one or two Parts.* . . Extra fcap. 8vo. 2s.

Juvenal. *XIII Satires.* Edited, with Introduction, Notes, etc., by C. H. PEARSON, M.A., and H. A. STRONG, M.A. . . . Crown 8vo. 6s.
                Or separately, Text and Introduction, 3s.; *Notes,* 3s. 6d.

Livy. *Selections* (for Schools). With Notes and Maps. By H. LEE-WARNER, M.A. . . . . Extra fcap. 8vo
    Part I. *The Caudine Disaster.* . . . . . . limp, 1s. 6d.
    Part II. *Hannibal's Campaign in Italy.* . . . . limp, 1s. 6d.
    Part III. *The Macedonian War.* . . . . . limp, 1s. 6d.

Livy. *Book I.* With Introduction, Historical Examination, and Notes. By J. R. SEELEY M.A. *Second Edition.* . . . . . 8vo. 6s.

Livy. *Books V—VII.* With Introduction and Notes. By A. R. CLUER, B.A. *Second Edition.* Revised by P. E. MATHESON, M.A. *In one or two parts.* . . . . Extra fcap. 8vo. 5s.

Livy. *Books XXI—XXIII.* With Introduction and Notes. By M. T. TATHAM, M.A. . . . . . . Extra fcap. 8vo. 4s. 6d.

Ovid. *Selections* (for the use of Schools). With Introductions and Notes, and an Appendix on the Roman Calendar. By W. RAMSAY, M.A. Edited by G. G. RAMSAY, M.A. *Third Edition.* . Extra fcap. 8vo. 5s. 6d.

Ovid. *Tristia,* Book I. Edited by S. G. OWEN, B.A.
Extra fcap. 8vo. 3s. 6d.

Persius. *The Satires.* With Translation and Commentary by J. CONINGTON, M.A., edited by H. NETTLESHIP, M.A. *Second Edition.*
8vo. 7s. 6d.

Plautus. *Captivi.* With Introduction and Notes. By W. M. LINDSAY, M.A. *In one or two Parts.* . . . . . Extra fcap. 8vo. 2s. 6d.

Plautus. *Trinummus.* With Notes and Introductions. By C. E. FREEMAN, M.A. and A. SLOMAN, M.A. . . . Extra fcap. 8vo. 3s.

Pliny. *Selected Letters* (for Schools). With Notes. By the late C. E. PRICHARD, M.A., and E. R. BERNARD, M.A. *New Edition. In one or two Parts.* . . . . Extra fcap. 8vo. 3s.

Sallust. *Bellum Catilinarium* and *Jugurthinum.* With Introduction and Notes, by W. W. CAPES, M.A. . . . Extra fcap. 8vo. 4s. 6d.

Tacitus. *The Annals.* Books I—IV. Edited, with Introduction and Notes for the use of Schools and Junior Students, by H. FURNEAUX, M.A.
Extra fcap. 8vo. 5s.

Tacitus. *The Annals.* Book I. By the same Editor.
Extra fcap. 8vo. *limp,* 2s.

Terence. *Adelphi.* With Notes and Introductions. By A. SLOMAN, M.A. . . . . Extra fcap. 8vo. 3s.

Terence. *Andria.* With Notes and Introductions. By C. E. FREEMAN, M.A., and A. SLOMAN, M.A. . . . . . Extra fcap. 8vo. 3s.

Terence. *Phormio.* With Notes and Introductions. By A. SLOMAN, M.A. . . . . Extra fcap. 8vo. 3s.

Tibullus and **Propertius.** Edited, with Introduction and Notes, by G. G. RAMSAY, M.A. *In one or two Parts.* . . . Extra fcap. 8vo. 6s.

Virgil. With Introduction and Notes, by T. L. PAPILLON, M.A. In Two Volumes. . . . Crown 8vo. 10s. 6d.; Text separately, 4s. 6d.

Virgil. *Bucolics.* With Introduction and Notes, by C. S. JERRAM, M.A.
In one or two Parts. Extra fcap. 8vo. 2s. 6d.

Virgil. *Aeneid I.* With Introduction and Notes, by C. S. JERRAM, M.A.
Extra fcap. 8vo. *limp,* 1s. 6d.

Virgil. *Aeneid IX.* Edited with Introduction and Notes, by A. E. HAIGH, M.A. . . . Extra fcap 8vo. *limp* 1s. 6d. *In two Parts.* 2s.

GREEK.

Chandler. *The Elements of Greek Accentuation* (for Schools). By H. W. CHANDLER, M.A. *Second Edition.* Extra fcap. 8vo. 2s. 6d.

Liddell and Scott. *A Greek-English Lexicon*, by HENRY GEORGE LIDDELL, D.D., and ROBERT SCOTT, D.D. *Seventh Edition.* 4to. 36s.

Liddell and Scott. *A Greek-English Lexicon*, abridged from LIDDELL and SCOTT's 4to. edition, chiefly for the use of Schools. *Twenty-first Edition.* Square 12mo. 7s. 6d.

Veitch. *Greek Verbs, Irregular and Defective*; their forms, meaning, and quantity; embracing all the Tenses used by Greek writers, with references to the passages in which they are found. By W. VEITCH, LL.D. *Fourth Edition.* Crown 8vo. 10s. 6d.

Wordsworth. *Graecae Grammaticae Rudimenta in usum Scholarum.* Auctore CAROLO WORDSWORTH, D.C.L. *Nineteenth Edition.* 12mo. 4s.

Wordsworth. *A Greek Primer, for the use of beginners in that Language.* By the Right Rev. CHARLES WORDSWORTH, D.C.L., Bishop of St. Andrew's. *Seventh Edition.* Extra fcap. 8vo. 1s. 6d.

Wright. *The Golden Treasury of Ancient Greek Poetry;* being a Collection of the finest passages in the Greek Classic Poets, with Introductory Notices and Notes. By R. S. WRIGHT, M.A. *New edition in the Press.*

Wright and Shadwell. *A Golden Treasury of Greek Prose;* being a Collection of the finest passages in the principal Greek Prose Writers, with Introductory Notices and Notes. By R. S. WRIGHT, M.A., and J. E. L. SHADWELL, M.A. Extra fcap. 8vo. 4s. 6d.

A SERIES OF GRADUATED READERS.—

Easy Greek Reader. By EVELYN ABBOTT, M.A. *In one or two Parts.* Extra fcap. 8vo. 3s.

First Greek Reader. By W. G. RUSHBROOKE, M.L., Second Classical Master at the City of London School. *Second Edition.* Extra fcap. 8vo. 2s. 6d.

Second Greek Reader. By A. M. BELL, M.A. Extra fcap. 8vo. 3s. 6d.

Fourth Greek Reader; being Specimens of Greek Dialects. With Introductions and Notes. By W. W. MERRY, D.D., Rector of Lincoln College. Extra fcap. 8vo. 4s. 6d.

Fifth Greek Reader. Selections from Greek Epic and Dramatic Poetry, with Introductions and Notes. By EVELYN ABBOTT, M.A. Extra fcap. 8vo. 4s. 6d.

THE GREEK TESTAMENT.—

Evangelia Sacra Graece. Fcap. 8vo. *limp,* 1s. 6d.

The Greek Testament, with the Readings adopted by the Revisers of the Authorised Version. Fcap. 8vo. 4s. 6d.; or on writing paper, with wide margin, 15s.

Novum Testamentum Graece juxta Exemplar Millianum. 18mo. 2s. 6d.; or on writing paper, with large margin, 9s.

Novum Testamentum Graece. Accedunt parallela S. Scripturae loca, necnon vetus capitulorum notatio et canones Eusebii. Edidit CAROLUS LLOYD, S.T.P.R., necnon Episcopus Oxoniensis.
18mo. 3s.; or on writing paper, with large margin, 10s. 6d.

The New Testament in Greek and English. Edited by E. CARDWELL, D.D. . . . . . . 2 vols. crown 8vo. 6s.

A Greek Testament Primer. An Easy Grammar and Reading Book for the use of Students beginning Greek. By REV. E. MILLER, M.A.
Extra fcap. 8vo. 3s. 6d.

Outlines of Textual Criticism applied to the New Testament. By C. E. HAMMOND, M.A. *Fourth Edition.* . . Extra fcap. 8vo. 3s. 6d.

Aeschylus. *Agamemnon.* With Introduction and Notes, by ARTHUR SIDGWICK, M.A. *Third Edition.* In one or two Parts . Extra fcap. 8vo. 3s.

Aeschylus. *Choephoroi.* With Introduction and Notes, by the same Editor. . . . . Extra fcap. 8vo. 3s.

Aeschylus. *Eumenides.* With Introduction and Notes, by the same Editor. *In one or two Parts.* . . . . . Extra fcap. 8vo. 3s.

Aeschylus. *Prometheus Bound.* With Introduction and Notes, by A. O. PRICKARD, M.A. *Second Edition.* . . . Extra fcap. 8vo. 2s.

Aristophanes. *The Clouds.* With Introduction and Notes, by W. W. MERRY, D.D. *Second Edition.* . . . . Extra fcap. 8vo. 2s.

Aristophanes. *The Acharnians.* By the same Editor. *Third Edition. In one or two Parts.* . . . . Extra fcap. 8vo. 3s.

Aristophanes. *The Frogs.* By the same Editor. *New Edition. In one or two Parts.* . . . . Extra fcap. 8vo. 3s.

Aristophanes. *The Knights.* By the same Editor. *In one or two Parts.* . . . . Extra fcap. 8vo. 3s.

Cebes. *Tabula.* With Introduction and Notes, by C. S. JERRAM, M.A.
Extra fcap. 8vo. 2s. 6d.

Demosthenes. *Orations against Philip.* With Introduction and Notes. By EVELYN ABBOTT, M.A., and P. E. MATHESON, M.A., Vol. I. *Philippic I and Olynthiacs I—III. In one or two Parts.* . . Extra fcap. 8vo. 3s.

Euripides. *Alcestis.* By C. S. JERRAM, M.A. Extra fcap. 8vo. 2s. 6d.

Euripides. *Helena.* By the same Editor. . Extra fcap. 8vo. 3s.

Euripides. *Iphigenia in Tauris.* With Introduction and Notes. By the same Editor. . . . . Extra fcap. 8vo. 3s.

Euripides. *Medea.* With Introduction, Notes and Appendices. By C. B. HEBERDEN, M.A. *In one or two Parts.* . . Extra fcap. 8vo. 2s.

Herodotus. Book IX. Edited with Notes, by EVELYN ABBOTT, M.A. *In one or two Parts.* . . . . . Extra fcap. 8vo. 3s.

Herodotus. *Selections.* Edited, with Introduction, Notes, and a Map, by W. W. MERRY, D.D. . . . . . Extra fcap. 8vo. 2s. 6d.

Homer. *Iliad,* Books I-XII. With an Introduction, a brief Homeric Grammar, and Notes. By D. B. MONRO, M.A. Extra fcap. 8vo. 6s.

Homer. *Iliad,* Book I. By the same Editor. *Third Edition.*
Extra fcap. 8vo. 2s.

Homer. *Iliad,* Books VI and XXI. With Notes, &c. By HERBERT HAILSTONE, M.A. . . . . . . Extra fcap. 8vo. 1s. 6d. each.

Homer. *Odyssey,* Books I–XII. By W. W. MERRY, D.D. *New Edition. In one or two Parts.* . . . . Extra fcap. 8vo. 5s.
Homer. *Odyssey,* Books XIII–XXIV. By the same Editor. *Second Edition.* . . . . Extra fcap. 8vo. 5s.
Homer. *Odyssey,* Books I and II. By the same Editor.
Extra fcap. 8vo. each 1s. 6d.
Lucian. *Vera Historia.* By C. S. JERRAM, M.A. *Second Edition.*
Extra fcap. 8vo. 1s. 6d.
Plato. *The Apology.* With a revised Text and English Notes, and a Digest of Platonic Idioms, by JAMES RIDDELL, M.A. . . 8vo. 8s. 6d.
Plato. *The Apology.* With Introduction and Notes. By ST. GEORGE STOCK, M.A. *In one or two Parts.* . . . . Extra fcap. 8vo. 2s. 6d.
Plato. *Meno.* With Introduction and Notes. By ST. GEORGE STOCK, M.A. *In one or two Parts.* . . . . . Extra fcap. 8vo. 2s. 6d.
Sophocles. (For the use of Schools.) Edited with Introductions and English Notes by LEWIS CAMPBELL, M.A., and EVELYN ABBOTT, M.A. New and Revised Edition. 2 Vols. . . . Extra fcap. 8vo. 10s. 6d.
Sold separately, Vol. I. Text, 4s. 6d. Vol. II. Notes, 6s.

☞ *Also in single Plays. Extra fcap. 8vo. limp,*
Oedipus Tyrannus, Philoctetes. New and Revised Edition, 2s. each.
Oedipus Coloneus, Antigone. 1s. 9d. each.
Ajax, Electra, Trachiniae. 2s. each.

Sophocles. *Oedipus Rex:* Dindorf's Text, with Notes by W. BASIL JONES, D.D., Lord Bishop of S. David's. . Extra fcap. 8vo. *limp,* 1s. 6d.
Theocritus. Edited, with Notes, by H. KYNASTON, D.D. (late SNOW), Head Master of Cheltenham College. *Fourth Edition.*
Extra fcap. 8vo. 4s. 6d.
Xenophon. *Easy Selections* (for Junior Classes). With a Vocabulary, Notes, and Map. By J. S. PHILLPOTTS, B.C.L., Head Master of Bedford School, and C. S. JERRAM, M.A. *Third Edition.* . Extra fcap. 8vo. 3s. 6d.
Xenophon. *Selections* (for Schools). With Notes and Maps. By J. S. PHILLPOTTS, B.C.L. *Fourth Edition.* . . Extra fcap. 8vo. 3s. 6d.
Xenophon. *Anabasis,* Book I. With Notes and Map. By J. MARSHALL, M.A., Rector of the High School, Edinburgh. . . Extra fcap. 8vo. 2s. 6d.
Xenophon. *Anabasis,* Book II. With Notes and Map. By C. S. JERRAM, M.A. . . . . Extra fcap. 8vo. 2s.
Xenophon. *Cyropaedia,* Books IV, V. With Introduction and Notes, by C. BIGG, D.D. . . . . Extra fcap. 8vo. 2s. 6d.

ENGLISH.

Reading Books.

—— *A First Reading Book.* By MARIE EICHENS of Berlin; edited by ANNE J. CLOUGH. . . . . . Extra fcap. 8vo. *stiff covers,* 4d.
—— *Oxford Reading Book,* Part I. For Little Children.
Extra fcap. 8vo. *stiff covers,* 6d.
—— *Oxford Reading Book,* Part II. For Junior Classes.
Extra fcap. 8vo. *stiff covers,* 6d.

LIST OF SCHOOL BOOKS. 7

Skeat. *A Concise Etymological Dictionary of the English Language.* By W. W. Skeat, Litt. D. *Third Edition.* . . . Crown 8vo. 5s. 6d.

Tancock. *An Elementary English Grammar and Exercise Book.* By O. W. Tancock, M.A., Head Master of King Edward VI's School, Norwich. *Second Edition.* . . . . Extra fcap. 8vo. 1s. 6d.

Tancock. *An English Grammar and Reading Book,* for Lower Forms in Classical Schools. By O. W. Tancock, M.A. *Fourth Edition.* Extra fcap. 8vo. 3s. 6d.

Skeat. *The Principles of English Etymology. First Series.* By W. W. Skeat, Litt. D. . . . . Crown 8vo. 9s.

Earle. *The Philology of the English Tongue.* By J. Earle, M.A., Professor of Anglo-Saxon. *Fourth Edition.* . . Extra fcap. 8vo. 7s. 6d.

Earle. *A Book for the Beginner in Anglo-Saxon.* By the same Author. *Third Edition.* . . . . Extra fcap. 8vo. 2s. 6d.

Sweet. *An Anglo-Saxon Primer, with Grammar, Notes, and Glossary.* By Henry Sweet, M.A. *Third Edition.* . . Extra fcap. 8vo. 2s. 6d.

Sweet. *An Anglo-Saxon Reader.* In Prose and Verse. With Grammatical Introduction, Notes, and Glossary. By the same Author. *Fourth Edition, Revised and Enlarged.* . . . . Extra fcap. 8vo. 8s. 6d.

Sweet. *A Second Anglo-Saxon Reader.* By the same Author.
Extra fcap. 8vo. 4s. 6d.

Sweet. *Anglo-Saxon Reading Primers.*
   I. *Selected Homilies of Ælfric.* Extra fcap. 8vo. *stiff covers,* 1s. 6d.
   II. *Extracts from Alfred's Orosius.* Extra fcap. 8vo. *stiff covers,* 1s. 6d.

Sweet. *First Middle English Primer, with Grammar and Glossary.* By the same Author. . . . . . Extra fcap. 8vo. 2s.

Sweet. *Second Middle English Primer.* Extracts from Chaucer, with Grammar and Glossary. By the same Author. . . Extra fcap. 8vo. 2s.

Morris and Skeat. *Specimens of Early English.* A New and Revised Edition. With Introduction, Notes, and Glossarial Index. By R. Morris, LL.D., and W. W. Skeat, Litt. D.
   Part I. From Old English Homilies to King Horn (A.D. 1150 to A.D. 1300). *Second Edition.* . . . . . . Extra fcap. 8vo. 9s.
   Part II. From Robert of Gloucester to Gower (A.D. 1298 to A.D. 1393). *Third Edition.* . . . . . . Extra fcap. 8vo. 7s. 6d.

Skeat. *Specimens of English Literature,* from the 'Ploughmans Crede' to the 'Shepheardes Calender' (A.D. 1394 to A.D. 1579). With Introduction, Notes, and Glossarial Index. By W. W. Skeat, Litt. D. *Fourth Edition.*
Extra fcap. 8vo. 7s. 6d.

Typical Selections from the best English Writers, with Introductory Notices. *Second Edition.* In Two Volumes. Vol. I. Latimer to Berkeley. Vol. II. Pope to Macaulay. . . Extra fcap. 8vo. 3s. 6d. each.

A SERIES OF ENGLISH CLASSICS.—

Langland. *The Vision of William concerning Piers the Plowman,* by William Langland. Edited by W. W. Skeat, Litt. D. *Fourth Edition.*
Extra fcap. 8vo. 4s. 6d.

Chaucer. I. *The Prologue to the Canterbury Tales; The Knightes Tale; The Nonne Prestes Tale.* Edited by R. Morris, LL.D. *Fifty-first Thousand.* . . . . Extra fcap. 8vo. 2s. 6d.

Chaucer. II. *The Prioresses Tale; Sir Thopas; The Monkes Tale; The Clerkes Tale; The Squieres Tale, &c.* Edited by W. W. SKEAT, Litt. D. Third Edition. . . . . Extra fcap. 8vo. 4s. 6d.

Chaucer. III. *The Tale of the Man of Lawe; The Pardoneres Tale; The Second Nonnes Tale; The Chanouns Yemannes Tale.* By the same Editor. *New Edition, Revised.* . . . . Extra fcap. 8vo. 4s. 6d.

Gamelyn, The Tale of. Edited by W. W. SKEAT, Litt. D.
Extra fcap. 8vo. *stiff covers*, 1s. 6d.

Minot. *The Poems of Laurence Minot.* Edited, with Introduction and Notes, by JOSEPH HALL, M.A. . . . Extra fcap. 8vo. 4s. 6d.

Wycliffe. *The New Testament in English*, according to the Version by JOHN WYCLIFFE, about A.D. 1380, and Revised by JOHN PURVEY, about A.D. 1388. With Introduction and Glossary by W. W. SKEAT, Litt. D.
Extra fcap. 8vo. 6s.

Wycliffe. *The Books of Job, Psalms, Proverbs, Ecclesiastes, and the Song of Solomon*: according to the Wycliffite Version made by NICHOLAS DE HEREFORD, about A.D. 1381, and Revised by JOHN PURVEY, about A.D. 1388. With Introduction and Glossary by W. W. SKEAT, Litt. D. Extra fcap. 8vo. 3s. 6d.

Spenser. *The Faery Queene.* Books I and II. Edited by G. W. KITCHIN, D.D.

    Book I. *Tenth Edition.* . . . . Extra fcap. 8vo. 2s. 6d.
    Book II. *Sixth Edition.* . . . . Extra fcap. 8vo. 2s. 6d.

Hooker. *Ecclesiastical Polity*, Book I. Edited by R. W. CHURCH, M.A., Dean of St. Paul's. *Second Edition.* . . . Extra fcap. 8vo. 2s.

Marlowe and Greene.—MARLOWE's *Tragical History of Dr. Faustus*, and GREENE's *Honourable History of Friar Bacon and Friar Bungay.* Edited by A. W. WARD, M.A. *Second Edition.* . Extra fcap. 8vo. 6s. 6d.

Marlowe. *Edward II.* Edited by O. W. TANCOCK, M.A. *Second Edition.* . . . . . Extra fcap. 8vo. *Paper covers*, 2s. *cloth*, 3s.

Shakespeare. Select Plays. Edited by W. G. CLARK, M.A., and W. ALDIS WRIGHT, M.A. . . . . Extra fcap. 8vo. *stiff covers*.

    The Merchant of Venice. 1s.   *Macbeth.* 1s. 6d.
    Richard the Second. 1s. 6d.   *Hamlet.* 2s.

        Edited by W. ALDIS WRIGHT, M.A.

    The Tempest. 1s. 6d.   *Coriolanus.* 2s. 6d.
    As You Like It. 1s. 6d.   *Richard the Third.* 2s. 6d.
    A Midsummer Night's Dream. 1s. 6d.   *Henry the Fifth.* 2s.
    Twelfth Night. 1s. 6d.   *King John.* 1s. 6d.
    Julius Cæsar. 2s.   *King Lear.* 1s. 6d.
        Henry the Eighth (in the Press).

Shakespeare as a Dramatic Artist; *a popular Illustration of the Principles of Scientific Criticism.* By RICHARD G. MOULTON, M.A.
Crown 8vo. 5s.

Bacon. I. *Advancement of Learning.* Edited by W. ALDIS WRIGHT, M.A. *Third Edition.* . . . . . Extra fcap. 8vo. 4s. 6d.

Bacon. II. *The Essays.* With Introduction and Notes. *In Preparation.*

LIST OF SCHOOL BOOKS. 9

Milton. I. *Areopagitica.* With Introduction and Notes. By John W. Hales, M.A. *Third Edition.* . . . . Extra fcap. 8vo. 3s.

Milton. II. *Poems.* Edited by R. C. Browne, M.A. 2 vols. *Fifth Edition.* . Extra fcap. 8vo. 6s. 6d. Sold separately, Vol. I. 4s., Vol. II. 3s.
In paper covers:—
Lycidas, 3d. *L'Allegro*, 3d. *Il Penseroso*, 4d. *Comus*, 6d.

Milton. III. *Paradise Lost.* Book I. Edited with Notes, by H. C. Beeching, M.A. . Extra fcap. 8vo. 1s. 6d. *In white Parchment*, 3s. 6d.

Milton. IV. *Samson Agonistes.* Edited with Introduction and Notes by John Churton Collins. . . . Extra fcap. 8vo. *stiff covers*, 1s.

Clarendon. *History of the Rebellion.* Book VI. Edited with Introduction and Notes by T. Arnold, M.A. . . Extra fcap. 8vo. 4s. 6d.

Bunyan. I. *The Pilgrim's Progress, Grace Abounding, Relation of the Imprisonment of Mr. John Bunyan.* Edited, with Biographical Introduction and Notes, by E. Venables, M.A.
Extra fcap. 8vo. 5s. *In white Parchment*, 6s.

Bunyan. II. *Holy War, &c.* By the same Editor. *In the Press.*

Dryden. *Select Poems.—Stanzas on the Death of Oliver Cromwell; Astræa Redux; Annus Mirabilis; Absalom and Achitophel; Religio Laici; The Hind and the Panther.* Edited by W. D. Christie, M.A.
Extra fcap. 8vo. 3s. 6d.

Locke's *Conduct of the Understanding.* Edited, with Introduction, Notes, &c. by T. Fowler, D.D. *Second Edition.* . . Extra fcap. 8vo. 2s.

Addison. *Selections from Papers in the 'Spectator.'* With Notes. By T. Arnold, M.A. . Extra fcap. 8vo. 4s. 6d. *In white Parchment*, 6s.

Steele. *Selected Essays from the Tatler, Spectator, and Guardian.* By Austin Dobson. . . Extra fcap. 8vo. 5s. *In white Parchment*, 7s. 6d.

Berkeley. *Select Works of Bishop Berkeley*, with an Introduction and Notes, by A. C. Fraser, LL.D. *Third Edition.* . . Crown 8vo. 7s. 6d.

Pope. I. *Essay on Man.* Edited by Mark Pattison, B.D. *Sixth Edition.* . . . . Extra fcap. 8vo. 1s. 6d.

Pope. II. *Satires and Epistles.* By the same Editor. *Second Edition.*
Extra fcap. 8vo. 2s.

Parnell. *The Hermit.* . . . . . *Paper covers*, 2d.

Johnson. I. *Rasselas; Lives of Dryden and Pope.* Edited by Alfred Milnes, M.A. . . . . . Extra fcap. 8vo. 4s. 6d.
Lives of Pope and Dryden. . . . . *Stiff covers*, 2s. 6d.

Johnson. II. *Rasselas.* Edited, with Introduction and Notes, by G. Birkbeck Hill, D.C.L. Extra fcap.8vo. *limp*, 2s. *In white Parchment*, 3s. 6d.

Johnson. III. *Vanity of Human Wishes.* With Notes, by E. J. Payne, M.A. . . . . *Paper covers*, 4d.

Johnson. IV. *Life of Milton.* Edited by C. H. Firth, M.A.
In the Press.

Gray. *Selected Poems.* Edited by EDMUND GOSSE.
Extra fcap. 8vo. *Stiff covers*, 1s. 6d. *In white Parchment*, 3s.

Gray. *Elegy, and Ode on Eton College.* . . . Paper covers, 2d.

Goldsmith. *Selected Poems.* Edited, with Introduction and Notes, by AUSTIN DOBSON. . . . . Extra fcap. 8vo. 3s. 6d.
In white Parchment, 4s. 6d.

The Deserted Village. . . . . Paper covers, 2d.

Cowper. I. *The Didactic Poems of* 1782, with Selections from the Minor Pieces, A.D. 1779-1783. Edited by H. T. GRIFFITH, B.A.
Extra fcap. 8vo. 3s.

Cowper. II. *The Task, with Tirocinium,* and Selections from the Minor Poems, A.D. 1784-1799. By the same Editor. *Second Edition.*
Extra fcap. 8vo. 3s.

Burke. I. *Thoughts on the Present Discontents; the two Speeches on America.* Edited by E. J. PAYNE, M.A. *Second Edition.*
Extra fcap. 8vo. 4s. 6d.

Burke. II. *Reflections on the French Revolution.* By the same Editor. *Second Edition.* . . . . . . Extra fcap. 8vo. 5s.

Burke. III. *Four Letters on the Proposals for Peace with the Regicide Directory of France.* By the same Editor. *Second Edition.*
Extra fcap. 8vo. 5s.

Keats. *Hyperion*, Book I. With Notes, by W. T. ARNOLD, B.A.
Paper covers, 4d.

Byron. *Childe Harold.* With Introduction and Notes, by H. F. TOZER, M.A. . . . . Extra fcap. 8vo. 3s. 6d. *In white Parchment*, 5s.

Scott. *Lay of the Last Minstrel.* Edited with Preface and Notes by W. MINTO, M.A. With Map.
Extra fcap. 8vo. *stiff covers*, 2s. *In Ornamental Parchment*, 3s. 6d.

Scott. *Lay of the Last Minstrel.* Introduction and Canto I, with Preface and Notes by W. MINTO, M.A. . . . . Paper covers, 6d.

FRENCH AND ITALIAN.

Brachet. *Etymological Dictionary of the French Language,* with a Preface on the Principles of French Etymology. Translated into English by G. W. KITCHIN, D.D., Dean of Winchester. *Third Edition.*
Crown 8vo. 7s. 6d.

Brachet. *Historical Grammar of the French Language.* Translated into English by G. W. KITCHIN, D.D. *Fourth Edition.*
Extra fcap. 8vo. 3s. 6d.

Saintsbury. *Primer of French Literature.* By GEORGE SAINTSBURY, M.A. *Second Edition.* . . . . . Extra fcap. 8vo. 2s.

Saintsbury. *Short History of French Literature.* By the same Author. . . . . Crown 8vo. 10s. 6d.

Saintsbury. *Specimens of French Literature.* . . Crown 8vo. 9s.

LIST OF SCHOOL BOOKS.

Beaumarchais. *Le Barbier de Séville.* With Introduction and Notes by AUSTIN DOBSON. . . . . . Extra fcap. 8vo. 2s. 6d.

Blouët. *L'Éloquence de la Chaire et de la Tribune Françaises.* Edited by PAUL BLOUËT, B.A. (Univ. Gallic.). Vol. I. *French Sacred Oratory.* Extra fcap. 8vo. 2s. 6d.

Corneille. *Horace.* With Introduction and Notes by GEORGE SAINTSBURY, M.A. . . . . . Extra fcap. 8vo. 2s. 6d.

Corneille. *Cinna.* With Notes, Glossary, etc. By GUSTAVE MASSON, B.A. . . . . . Extra fcap. 8vo. *stiff covers*, 1s. 6d. *cloth*, 2s.

Gautier (Théophile). *Scenes of Travel.* Selected and Edited by G. SAINTSBURY, M.A. . . . . . Extra fcap. 8vo. 2s.

Masson. *Louis XIV and his Contemporaries;* as described in Extracts from the best Memoirs of the Seventeenth Century. With English Notes, Genealogical Tables, &c. By GUSTAVE MASSON, B.A. Extra fcap. 8vo. 2s. 6d.

Molière. *Les Précieuses Ridicules.* With Introduction and Notes by ANDREW LANG, M.A. . . . . . Extra fcap. 8vo. 1s. 6d.

Molière. *Les Femmes Savantes.* With Notes, Glossary, etc. By GUSTAVE MASSON, B.A. . Extra fcap. 8vo. *stiff covers*, 1s. 6d. *cloth*, 2s.

Molière. *Les Fourberies de Scapin.* } With Voltaire's Life of Molière. By
Racine. *Athalie.* } GUSTAVE MASSON, B.A. Extra fcap. 8vo. 2s. 6d.

Molière. *Les Fourberies de Scapin.* With Voltaire's Life of Molière. By GUSTAVE MASSON, B.A. . . Extra fcap. 8vo. *stiff covers*, 1s. 6d.

Musset. *On ne badine pas avec l'Amour,* and *Fantasio.* With Introduction, Notes, etc., by WALTER HERRIES POLLOCK. Extra fcap. 8vo. 2s.

NOVELETTES :—

Xavier de Maistre. *Voyage autour de ma Chambre.* ⎫
Madame de Duras. *Ourika.* ⎪ By GUSTAVE
Erckmann-Chatrian. *Le Vieux Tailleur.* ⎬ MASSON, B.A., 3rd Edition
Alfred de Vigny. *La Veillée de Vincennes.* ⎪ Ext. fcap. 8vo.
Edmond About. *Les Jumeaux de l'Hôtel Corneille.* ⎪ 2s. 6d.
Rodolphe Töpffer. *Mésaventures d'un Écolier.* ⎭

Voyage autour de ma Chambre, separately, limp, 1s. 6d.

Quinet. *Lettres à sa Mère.* Edited by G. SAINTSBURY, M.A. Extra fcap. 8vo. 2s.

Racine. *Esther.* Edited by G. SAINTSBURY, M.A. Extra fcap. 8vo. 2s.

Racine. *Andromaque.* } With Louis Racine's Life of his Father. By
Corneille. *Le Menteur.* } GUSTAVE MASSON, B.A. Extra fcap. 8vo. 2s. 6d.

Regnard. . . . *Le Joueur.* } By GUSTAVE MASSON, B.A.
Brueys and Palaprat. *Le Grondeur.* } Extra fcap. 8vo. 2s. 6d.

Sainte-Beuve. *Selections from the Causeries du Lundi.* Edited by G. SAINTSBURY, M.A. . . . . . . Extra fcap. 8vo. 2s.

Sévigné. *Selections from the Correspondence of* **Madame de Sévigné** and her chief Contemporaries. Intended more especially for Girls' Schools. By GUSTAVE MASSON, B.A. . . . . . Extra fcap. 8vo. 3s.

Voltaire. *Mérope.* Edited by G. SAINTSBURY, M.A. Extra fcap. 8vo. 2s.

Dante. *Selections from the 'Inferno.'* With Introduction and Notes, by H. B. COTTERILL, B.A. . . . . Extra fcap. 8vo. 4s. 6d.

Tasso. *La Gerusalemme Liberata.* Cantos i, ii. With Introduction and Notes, by the same Editor. . . . . Extra fcap. 8vo. 2s. 6d.

GERMAN, GOTHIC, ICELANDIC, &c.

Buchheim. *Modern German Reader.* A Graduated Collection of Extracts in Prose and Poetry from Modern German writers. Edited by C. A. BUCHHEIM, Phil. Doc.
    Part I. With English Notes, a Grammatical Appendix, and a complete Vocabulary. *Fourth Edition.* . . . Extra fcap. 8vo. 2s. 6d.
    Part II. With English Notes and an Index. Extra fcap. 8vo. 2s. 6d.
    Part III. In preparation.

Lange. *The Germans at Home*; a Practical Introduction to German Conversation, with an Appendix containing the Essentials of German Grammar. By HERMANN LANGE. *Third Edition.* . . . . . 8vo. 2s. 6d.

Lange. *The German Manual*; a German Grammar, a Reading Book, and a Handbook of German Conversation. By the same Author.
                                                                        8vo. 7s. 6d.

Lange. *A Grammar of the German Language,* being a reprint of the Grammar contained in *The German Manual.* By the same Author. 8vo. 3s. 6d.

Lange. *German Composition*; a Theoretical and Practical Guide to the Art of Translating English Prose into German. By the same Author. *Second Edition* . . . . 8vo. 4s. 6d.
        [*A Key in Preparation.*]

Lange. *German Spelling*: A Synopsis of the Changes which it has undergone through the Government Regulations of 1880 . *Paper cover, 6d.*

Becker's Friedrich der Grosse. With an Historical Sketch of the Rise of Prussia and of the Times of Frederick the Great. With Map. Edited by C. A. BUCHHEIM, Phil. Doc. . . . Extra fcap. 8vo. 3s. 6d.

Goethe. *Egmont.* With a Life of Goethe, etc. Edited by C. A. BUCHHEIM, Phil. Doc. *Third Edition.* . . . Extra fcap. 8vo. 3s.

Goethe. *Iphigenie auf Tauris.* A Drama. With a Critical Introduction and Notes. Edited by C. A. BUCHHEIM, Phil. Doc. *Second Edition.* Extra fcap. 8vo. 3s.

Heine's *Harzreise.* With a Life of Heine, etc. Edited by C. A. BUCHHEIM, Phil. Doc. Extra fcap. 8vo. *stiff covers*, 1s. 6d. *cloth*, 2s. 6d.

LIST OF SCHOOL BOOKS. 13

Heine's *Prosa,* being Selections from his Prose Works. Edited with English Notes, etc., by C. A. BUCHHEIM, Phil. Doc. Extra fcap. 8vo. 4s. 6d.

Lessing. *Laokoon.* With Introduction, Notes, etc. By A. HAMANN, Phil. Doc., M.A. Extra fcap. 8vo. 4s. 6d.

Lessing. *Minna von Barnhelm.* A Comedy. With a Life of Lessing, Critical Analysis, Complete Commentary, etc. Edited by C. A. BUCHHEIM, Phil. Doc. *Fifth Edition.* Extra fcap. 8vo. 3s. 6d.

Lessing. *Nathan der Weise.* With English Notes, etc. Edited by C. A. BUCHHEIM, Phil. Doc. *Second Edition.* Extra fcap. 8vo. 4s. 6d.

Niebuhr's *Griechische Heroen-Geschichten.* Tales of Greek Heroes. Edited with English Notes and a Vocabulary, by EMMA S. BUCHHEIM. Extra fcap. 8vo. *cloth,* 2s.

Schiller's *Historische Skizzen:—Egmonts Leben und Tod,* and *Belagerung von Antwerpen.* Edited by C. A. BUCHHEIM, Phil. Doc. *Third Edition, Revised and Enlarged, with a Map.* Extra fcap. 8vo. 2s. 6d.

Schiller. *Wilhelm Tell.* With a Life of Schiller; an Historical and Critical Introduction, Arguments, a Complete Commentary, and Map. Edited by C. A. BUCHHEIM, Phil. Doc. *Sixth Edition.* Extra fcap. 8vo. 3s. 6d.

Schiller. *Wilhelm Tell.* Edited by C. A. BUCHHEIM, Phil. Doc. *School Edition.* With Map. Extra fcap. 8vo. 2s.

Schiller. *Wilhelm Tell.* Translated into English Verse by E. MASSIE, M.A. Extra fcap. 8vo. 5s.

Schiller. *Die Jungfrau von Orleans.* Edited by C. A. BUCHHEIM, Phil. Doc. [*In preparation.*]

Scherer. *A History of German Literature.* By W. SCHERER. Translated from the Third German Edition by Mrs. F. CONYBEARE. Edited by F. MAX MÜLLER. 2 vols. 8vo. 21s.

Max Müller. *The German Classics from the Fourth to the Nineteenth Century.* With Biographical Notices, Translations into Modern German, and Notes, by F. MAX MÜLLER, M.A. A New edition, revised, enlarged, and adapted to WILHELM SCHERER's *History of German Literature,* by F. LICHTENSTEIN. 2 vols. Crown 8vo. 21s.

Wright. *A Middle High German Primer.* With Grammar, Notes, and Glossary. By JOSEPH WRIGHT, Ph. D. *Extra fcap.* 8vo. 3s. 6d.

Skeat. *The Gospel of St. Mark in Gothic.* Edited by W. W. SKEAT, Litt. D. Extra fcap. 8vo. 4s.

Sweet. An Icelandic Primer, with Grammar, Notes, and Glossary. By HENRY SWEET, M.A. Extra fcap. 8vo. 3s. 6d.

Vigfusson and Powell. *An Icelandic Prose Reader,* with Notes, Grammar, and Glossary. By GUDBRAND VIGFUSSON, M.A., and F. YORK POWELL, M.A. Extra fcap. 8vo. 10s. 6d.

MATHEMATICS AND PHYSICAL SCIENCE.

Aldis. *A Text Book of Algebra (with Answers to the Examples).* By W. STEADMAN ALDIS, M.A. . . . . . . Crown 8vo. 7s. 6d.

Hamilton and Ball. *Book-keeping.* By Sir R. G. C. HAMILTON, K.C.B., and JOHN BALL (of the firm of Quilter, Ball, & Co.). *New and Enlarged Edition* . . . . Extra fcap. 8vo. 2s.
*** *Ruled Exercise Books adapted to the above.* (Fcap. folio, 2s.)

Hensley. *Figures made Easy: a first Arithmetic Book.* By LEWIS HENSLEY, M.A. . . . . Crown 8vo. 6d.

Hensley. *Answers to the Examples in Figures made Easy*, together with 2000 additional Examples formed from the Tables in the same, with Answers. By the same Author. . . . . . Crown 8vo. 1s.

Hensley. *The Scholar's Arithmetic.* By the same Author.
Crown 8vo. 2s. 6d.

Hensley. *Answers to the Examples in the Scholar's Arithmetic.* By the same Author. . . . . Crown 8vo. 1s. 6d.

Hensley. *The Scholar's Algebra.* An Introductory work on Algebra. By the same Author. . . . . . . Crown 8vo. 2s. 6d.

Baynes. *Lessons on Thermodynamics.* By R. E. BAYNES, M.A., Lee's Reader in Physics. . . . . Crown 8vo. 7s. 6d.

Donkin. *Acoustics.* By W. F. DONKIN, M.A., F.R.S. *Second Edition.*
Crown 8vo. 7s. 6d.

Euclid Revised. Containing the essentials of the Elements of Plane Geometry as given by Euclid in his First Six Books. Edited by R. C. J. NIXON, M.A. . . . . Crown 8vo. 7s. 6d.
May likewise be had in parts as follows:—
Book I, 1s. Books I, II, 1s. 6d. Books I-IV, 3s. 6d. Books V-IV, 3s.

Euclid. *Geometry in Space.* Containing parts of Euclid's Eleventh and Twelfth Books. By the same Editor. . . . Crown 8vo. 3s. 6d.

Harcourt and Madan. *Exercises in Practical Chemistry.* Vol. I. *Elementary Exercises.* By A. G. VERNON HARCOURT, M.A.: and H. G. MADAN, M.A. *Fourth Edition.* Revised by H. G. Madan, M.A.
Crown 8vo. 10s. 6d.

Madan. *Tables of Qualitative Analysis.* Arranged by H. G. MADAN, M.A. . . . . Large 4to. 4s. 6d.

Maxwell. *An Elementary Treatise on Electricity.* By J. CLERK MAXWELL, M.A., F.R.S. Edited by W. GARNETT, M.A. Demy 8vo. 7s. 6d.

Stewart. *A Treatise on Heat*, with numerous Woodcuts and Diagrams. By BALFOUR STEWART, LL.D., F.R.S., Professor of Natural Philosophy in Owens College, Manchester. *Fifth Edition.* . Extra fcap. 8vo. 7s. 6d.

LIST OF SCHOOL BOOKS. 15

Williamson. *Chemistry for Students.* By A. W. WILLIAMSON, Phil. Doc., F.R.S., Professor of Chemistry, University College London. *A new Edition with Solutions.* . . . . . . Extra fcap. 8vo. 8s. 6d.

Combination Chemical Labels. In two Parts, gummed ready for use. Part I, Basic Radicals and Names of Elements. Part II, Acid Radicals. Price 3s. 6d.

HISTORY, POLITICAL ECONOMY, GEOGRAPHY, &c.

Danson. The Wealth of Households. By J. T. DANSON. Cr. 8vo. 5s.

Freeman. *A Short History of the Norman Conquest of England.* By E. A. FREEMAN, M.A. *Second Edition.* . Extra fcap. 8vo. 2s. 6d.

George. *Genealogical Tables illustrative of Modern History.* By H. B. GEORGE, M.A. *Third Edition, Revised and Enlarged.* Small 4to. 12s.

Hughes (Alfred). *Geography for Schools.* Part I, *Practical Geography.* With Diagrams. . . . . Extra fcap. 8vo. 2s. 6d.

Kitchin. *A History of France.* With Numerous Maps, Plans, and Tables. By G. W. KITCHIN, D.D., Dean of Winchester. *Second Edition.* Vol. I. To 1453. Vol. II. 1453-1624. Vol. III. 1624-1793. each 10s. 6d.

Lucas. *Introduction to a Historical Geography of the British Colonies.* By C. P. LUCAS, B.A. . . . . Crown 8vo., with 8 maps, 4s. 6d.

Rawlinson. *A Manual of Ancient History.* By G. RAWLINSON, M.A., Camden Professor of Ancient History. *Second Edition.* Demy 8vo. 14s.

Rogers. *A Manual of Political Economy,* for the use of Schools. By J. E. THOROLD ROGERS, M.A. *Third Edition.* Extra fcap. 8vo. 4s. 6d.

Stubbs. *The Constitutional History of England, in its Origin and Development.* By WILLIAM STUBBS, D.D., Lord Bishop of Chester. Three vols. . . . . Crown 8vo. each 12s.

Stubbs. *Select Charters and other Illustrations of English Constitutional History,* from the Earliest Times to the Reign of Edward I. Arranged and edited by W. STUBBS, D.D. *Fourth Edition.* Crown 8vo. 8s. 6d.

Stubbs. *Magna Carta*: a careful reprint. . . . 4to. *stitched,* 1s.

ART.

Hullah. *The Cultivation of the Speaking Voice.* By JOHN HULLAH. Extra fcap. 8vo. 2s. 6d.

Maclaren. *A System of Physical Education: Theoretical and Practical.* With 346 Illustrations drawn by A. MACDONALD, of the Oxford School of Art. By ARCHIBALD MACLAREN, the Gymnasium, Oxford. *Second Edition.* Extra fcap. 8vo. 7s. 6d.

Troutbeck and Dale. *A Music Primer for Schools.* By J. TROUTBECK, D.D., formerly Music Master in Westminster School, and R. F. DALE, M.A., B. Mus., late Assistant Master in Westminster School. Crown 8vo. 1s. 6d.

Tyrwhitt. *A Handbook of Pictorial Art.* By R. St. J. TYRWHITT, M.A. With coloured Illustrations, Photographs, and a chapter on Perspective, by A. MACDONALD. *Second Edition.* . . . 8vo. *half morocco*, 18s.

Upcott. *An Introduction to Greek Sculpture.* By L. E. UPCOTT, M.A. . . . . Crown 8vo. 4s. 6d.

Student's Handbook to the University and Colleges of Oxford. *Ninth Edition.* . . . . Crown 8vo. 2s. 6d.

Helps to the Study of the Bible, taken from the *Oxford Bible for Teachers*, comprising Summaries of the several Books, with copious Explanatory Notes and Tables illustrative of Scripture History and the Characteristics of Bible Lands; with a complete Index of Subjects, a Concordance, a Dictionary of Proper Names, and a series of Maps. . . . . Crown 8vo. 3s. 6d.

*** A READING ROOM *has been opened at the* CLARENDON PRESS WAREHOUSE, AMEN CORNER, *where visitors will find every facility for examining old and new works issued from the Press, and for consulting all official publications.*

☞ *All communications relating to Books included in this List, and offers of new Books and new Editions, should be addressed to*

THE SECRETARY TO THE DELEGATES,
CLARENDON PRESS,
OXFORD.

London : HENRY FROWDE,
OXFORD UNIVERSITY PRESS WAREHOUSE, AMEN CORNER.
Edinburgh : 6 QUEEN STREET.
Oxford : CLARENDON PRESS DEPOSITORY,
116 HIGH STREET.

www.ingramcontent.com/pod-product-compliance
Lightning Source LLC
Chambersburg PA
CBHW020304090426
42735CB00009B/1212